Band of
Brothers

*To the members of
Nineteen Mess, Grenville Division,
January to December 1947*

Band of Brothers

BOY SEAMEN IN THE ROYAL NAVY

David Phillipson

SUTTON PUBLISHING

This book was first published in 1996 by
Sutton Publishing Limited · Phoenix Mill
Thrupp · Stroud · Gloucestershire · GL5 2BU

This edition first published in 2003

British Library Cataloguing in Publication Data
A catalogue record for this book is available from the British
Library.

ISBN 0 7509 3181 7

Typeset in 11/12pt Photina.
Typesetting and origination by
Suttton Publishing Limited.
Printed and bound in Great Britain by
J.H. Haynes & Co. Ltd, Sparkford.

Contents

Chief Petty Officer Blenkinsop, 'The Black Angel', poses with his Leading Boys. The faint rictus discernible is a smile. Left to right: Pete Salkeld, Fred Blake, Chief Blenkinsop, Bob Harwood, Roy Coombes.

List of Plates

Acknowledgements

My thanks are due first and foremost to Mr Henry Baynham for allowing me to make extensive use in the early chapters of this book of the scholarly researches which went into his own authoritative and immensely readable naval histories. His kindness and helpful advice have greatly smoothed my path.

Thanks also to Chris Gray and John Delaney of the National Maritime and Imperial War Museums respectively, and to their staffs, for help with the illustrations. Also to Mrs Jacqueline McCutcheon of the Ministry of Defence Crown Copyright Office.

Acknowledgement is duly made to Messrs Hutchinson for permission to quote from Mr Baynham's works, and to Sampson Low and Marston Ltd of London and G. Chamberlain, Portsmouth, for other quotations attributed in the chapter end-notes. I have also drawn briefly on Mr Richard Baker's biography of Admiral of the Fleet Sir Michael Le Fanu, *Dry Ginger* (W.H. Allen, 1977) and Mr Alan Coles' *Invergordon Scapegoat* (Alan Sutton, 1993), a biography of Admiral Tomkinson. Every effort has been made to trace the copyright holders of all the quoted passages. The author would be pleased to rectify any omissions in future editions.

I am grateful to Jonathan Falconer, Anne Bennett and Melanie Leggett of Sutton Publishing for their help and patience.

David Phillipson
Biggin by Hulland
Derbyshire

Introduction

One day soon after the end of the Second World War, in the company of a male relative of middle years, I was strolling down the main thoroughfare of the smallish and undistinguished Midlands town in which I was brought up when I espied a youth of about my own age, dressed in sailor's uniform. This well-set-up lad with his careless, self-confident air cut a dashing figure. He wore on his sleeve a chevron of red worsted surmounted by a small anchor and a royal crown. The ribbon round his jaunty cap bore in gold letters, not the risible 'Sea Cadet Corps' but HMS *Ganges*, which signified that this young fellow was a real sailor, in the Navy.

How I envied him! Throughout my wartime childhood, spent as far from salt water as it is possible in England to live, while my school-mates to a boy were RAF-mad and could recite the specifications of every aircraft flown by that glamorous arm, I was the lone protagonist of the Silent Service, avid collector of every publication about the Royal Navy ever issued by the Ministry of Information and enthusiastic member of a Sea Scout troop which enjoyed honorary membership of the local rowing club. I had long ago determined to join the Navy just as soon as I was old enough. My school history master would jocularly address me as 'Lord Nelson' which caused merriment in the class and brought a flush of gratification to my cheek.

I made to accost this alluring figure to request information, but was led away by my companion, who warned: 'You don't want to talk to him, he's been a bad boy.'

Now it was true at that date that a juvenile court magistrate might suggest to a particular young offender brought before him that 'the Navy would make a man of you, my lad', and hint that he might prefer it to reform school. This actually occurred very infrequently, and less than 1 per cent of the Navy's juvenile intake came to it via the courts. But the calumny persisted, especially among the older land-locked, that any youngster in naval uniform must have been a 'bad boy'.

Undeterred and soon enough, I achieved my ambition and found myself in a round sailor's cap with HMS *Ganges* on the ribbon, numb with what would now be called culture shock.

HMS *Ganges* was the ship-name of the Royal Navy's principal boys' training establishment at Shotley Point near Ipswich. It was the first of the 'stone-frigates' built to replace the old training-hulks and was opened on 4 October 1905, in time to play its part in providing manpower for the vast expansion of the Fleet as the Dreadnoughts came into service. When I arrived within its close confines upwards of forty years, two world wars and a social revolution later, Shotley Barracks and what went on there was little known to the world outside but was a legend within the Navy, where its alumni were regarded with something approaching awe. I refer to *Ganges* elsewhere as a Victorian time-capsule embedded in the post-atomic Royal Navy; such it was, and such it was to remain until social pressures and a new broom brought about changes, six years after my drafting to the Fleet. The biographer of a Captain of *Ganges* and future First Sea Lord wrote:

> Arguably the most feudal of all the Navy's institutions was . . . HMS 'Ganges', the training establishment for new entrants, situated on the Suffolk coast at the junction of the rivers Stour and Orwell. Generations of young lads, separated for the first time from home and parents, made their first acquaintance with the Navy in this place. Many of them hated it, and most found it hard at first to come to terms with Naval routine . . . the treatment the boys received . . . would probably have been little different had the year been 1914.

The author is here referring to the mid-1950s. It is precisely the extraordinary conservatism with which the Royal Navy treated its young recruits that I have set out to chronicle in this book; one that I have itched to write for many years.

The British navy had employed boys in its ships for centuries, as the early chapters record. How little their portion improved down all those years, I am content for the reader to judge.

ONE

Wooden Walls

Why and how did young boys go to sea? The extreme youth of ships' boys in the eighteenth and early nineteenth centuries is more a cause for wonder to us today than it was then. The fact that a ten or twelve-year-old would leave his home to go to sea would have been taken for granted for two reasons: sons of any but wealthy parents did start work at that age, especially in rural communities; the country lad was set to work on the land, the boy growing up on the coast looked to the sea for his living. The second reason was that a seaman needed to start young to – literally – 'learn the ropes'; and there was much to learn. Thus the ship's boy, whether in man-of-war or merchant ship, became a competent and experienced seaman while still young, strong and agile. Also, many boys and young men were keen to go for a sailor; seafaring was an esoteric trade to the landsman who knew little of its harsh realities, and Jack Tar was a much-romanticized figure. Add to this the pay – an able seaman in the Navy received 24 shillings a month compared to the ploughman's £4 a year – and the prospect of prize money, of which even boys got a modest share, and it can be seen that a sailor's life had its attractions for a farm-boy.

In the mid-eighteenth century there was no such rating as 'boy' in the Royal Navy. Boys aged anything from nine to seventeen were entered on ships' books as 'servants'. This is a misnomer, or at least misleading, as the boys were not usually servants in the sense of domestics but were rather apprentice seamen. Servants formed an important part of a ship's company, sometimes amounting to between 12 and 15 per cent of authorized complement, though it was more usually about 8 per cent. Every commissioned officer was entitled to a servant (there might be as many as six lieutenants in a line-of-battle ship) while the 'standing officers'[1] – boatswain, gunner and carpenter – were allowed two each; the cook one and the captain four servants for every hundred crew on the ship's books.

The rating of servant is difficult to define. They came from a wide variety of social backgrounds and their aspirations varied as greatly. Some were young gentlemen, taken aboard by the captain at the request of their parents and usually for a consideration, to train as sea-officers. Their situation was usually implicitly recognized by a berth in the gunroom with the midshipmen and master's mates, or at least by being suffered to 'walk the quarterdeck'. The warrant officers' servants were similar to indentured apprentices ashore, learning their masters' trades with some prospect of preferment and a warrant of their own eventually. By far the largest number of servants aspired to nothing more than an able seaman's berth, with the possibility of advancement to petty officer. This last category included those who were the forerunners of the modern Boy Seamen with whom this book is concerned.

Throughout the eighteenth century social distinctions among a warship's company were much less rigid than they were to become in later periods. All naval officers, commissioned or warrant, had begun their careers on the lower deck. A candidate for commission as lieutenant was required to have served six years at sea, including two years as midshipman or master's mate. The other four years might be served in any lower rating – able seaman, ordinary seaman or even landman – wherever a vacancy happened to exist within the authorized complement. Such ratings during an aspirant officer's career were meaningless as he worked towards his goal, gaining the skills in seamanship, sail-handling and rigging which were an important part of a sea-officer's training. This mingling and intimate association of officer-candidates with common seamen helped to blur social distinctions (as apart from professional ones) between quarterdeck and lower deck. It was very much easier for a lower-middle-class boy, given that he had had some schooling, to achieve a lieutenant's commission, albeit after many year's service, than it was to become in a later age.

The ordinary run of boy volunteers sometimes came of seafaring families (though these were more likely to enter the merchant service); more often they were waifs or runaways. They were more likely to be from urban than rural areas, where ploughboys were in demand. An important source of recruitment during this period was the Marine Society, a philanthropic institution founded in 1756, which took in unwanted boys, waifs and strays (but not juvenile criminals); fed and housed them, taught them to read and write and gave them a smattering of seamanship before finding them a sea-going berth, more often in the merchant service than the Navy. Nevertheless, during the Seven Years War the Marine Society supplied the king's service with 10,625 recruits, about 5 per cent of the total needed. Admiral Boscawen, commanding the North America squadron, declared: 'No scheme for the manning of the Navy within my knowledge has ever had the success of the Marine Society.' This admirable organization accordingly performed a great patriotic service as well as a humanitarian one in rescuing and nurturing derelict children.

Unlike later, when men and boys on shipboard were strictly segregated, boys in the Georgian Navy lacking a more privileged berth were lumped in with the seamen, victualled in a broadside mess and slung their hammocks among them on the gun-deck. They were employed on such deck duties as their age and strength allowed. The smartest of the older boys worked aloft on the highest yards, the royals and topgallants, whose sails were the smallest and lightest. Some of these 'upperyardmen', who included potential officers,[2] were killed in falls, an occupational hazard for all seamen, but those who survived the experience gained valuable skill and confidence in working aloft. The Admiralty enjoined that all boys should be exercised in bending and reefing sails daily, and should compete with other ships in performing drills smartly. In ships with a captain who took an interest in the welfare and training of boys, of which there were regrettably few, the youngest of them enjoyed the benefit of a 'sea-daddy', an experienced seaman charged with the responsibility of looking after the boy; showing him how to prepare his food and mend his clothing as well as teaching him seamanship and the ways of the Navy, until he was old enough to stand on his own feet. Collingwood was such a captain: he, first among Nelson's 'band of brothers', was sympathetic to the plight of boys, having himself gone to sea at the age of eleven in 1762.

Sea-daddies aside, it was not a sheltered life for boys of tender years, and one can only wonder about their moral welfare, living as they did among rough seamen in the closely packed, promiscuous conditions of a man-of-war's 'tween-deck. This is not to hint at sexual debauchery; no doubt there was some but sodomy was the one capital offence in the old Navy for which, on conviction, the sentence was invariably carried out. Moral corruption was more likely from another source. Warships spent months, sometimes years, at sea without putting in to port, and when this became necessary most captains were loth to grant their people shore leave, given the virtual certainty that many of them would 'run'. Instead, a captain might permit boat-loads of women to be brought off for the indulgence of his crew during the time in port. An instance is recorded[3] of a frigate returning to Plymouth from the Brest blockade after a year at sea. The ship had a crew of 307; on the first morning in port the First Lieutenant counted the women on board and found them to number 309. Grog was freely issued on such occasions, and the scene below decks must have beggared description, certainly destroying any lingering innocence in a young boy's mind.[4] The scene is in fact described in a statement dated 1821, quoting

the shocking, disgraceful actions of the lower deck . . . the dirt, filth and stench; the disgusting conversation; the indecent, beastly conduct and horrible scenes; the blasphemy and swearing; the riots, quarrels and fighting; where hundreds of men and women are huddled together in one room and must be the witness of each other's actions . . . a ship in this state is justly termed by the more decent seamen 'a hell afloat'.

The officers were no better; the same report states: 'The lieutenants and grown midshipmen were allowed to have women in their respective mess-rooms, where the younger midshipmen were obliged to sit at table and associate with them, and to be witnesses of the debauchery and indecency which took place. It was even common for the women to employ all their arts to debauch these youths . . .'.

Parents, fortunately perhaps, like most of the population ashore, were ignorant of the details of naval life. An insight into the hardships of the blockade is given by a boy named Bernard Coleridge in a letter to his father and mother. He was aged eleven when his ship was blockading Brest in 1804.

Indeed we live on beef which has been ten or eleven years in corn and on biscuit which quite makes your throat cold in eating it owing to the maggots which are very cold when you eat them, like calves-foot jelly or blomonge being very fat indeed. Indeed, I do like this life very much but I cannot help laughing heartily when I think of sculling about the cyder-tub in the pond, and Mary Anne Cosserat capsizing into the pond just by the mulberry bush. I often think what I would give for two or three quarendons off the tree on the lawn with their rosy cheeks! We drink water the colour of the bark of a pear-tree with plenty of little maggots and weavils in it and wine which is exactly like bullock's blood and sawdust mixed together. I hope I shall not learn to swear, and by God's assistance I hope I shall not.[5]

Here we read a boy's mischievous delight in alarming his parents with lurid and probably exaggerated descriptions of his fare, a lightly-expressed admission of homesickness and an assurance for their concern at his learning bad habits from the men. The echo of this small voice down the years is made the more poignant when we learn that young Coleridge was killed in a fall from aloft at the age of fourteen.

As well as handling sails and rigging, the naval seamen manned the guns on the rare occasions when a battle offered. Every officer and man, boys included, had his place of duty in a gun action, and endless drills and practices were performed during the tedious months and years of blockade. Such was the British Tar's lot throughout much of the eighteenth century and well into the nineteenth – ceaseless cruising to and fro off an enemy coast, in all weathers and usually beyond sight of land, with no hope of a run ashore, longing for a fight to relieve the monotony. The Seven Years War, the War of Independence, the Revolutionary and Napoleonic Wars, with the enemy generally the French – all provided at least one major sea-battle and numerous lesser encounters, until the final decider of Trafalgar.

Before a battle, the gun-decks were cleared for action. Loose gear was stowed, hammocks removed to the upper deck and packed in nettings around the bulwarks as some protection from splinters and musket balls; mess tables were triced up to the deckheads. Casks of water were lashed to the 'tween-deck stanchions to douse fires and slake the ferocious thirst of the gunners: boys were responsible for keeping these replenished. One or two boys were detailed to each gun, with the duty of fetching powder from the magazine. Immediately above the magazine was the handling room, where the gunners' mates made up the powder into cartridges. Boys collected the cartridges in lidded leather pouches and ran with them to their respective guns. Those serving guns furthest from the magazine ran the hardest. A detailed and vivid account of boys at action stations is given by Samuel Leech in his memoirs, published much later in 1843. He was aged fourteen at the time of a fight with a United States frigate in the war of 1812:

> My station was at the fifth gun on the main deck. It was my duty to supply my gun with powder, a boy being appointed to each gun on the ship on the side we engaged for this purpose. A wooden screen was placed before the entrance to the magazine with a hole in it, through which the cartridges were passed to the boys; we received them there, and covering them with our coats, hurried to our respective guns. These precautions are observed to prevent the powder taking fire before it reaches the gun.

Action was joined:

> A strange noise, such as I had never heard before, next arrested my attention; it sounded like the tearing of sails, just over our heads. This I soon ascertained to be the wind of the enemy's shot. The roaring of cannon could now be heard from all parts of our trembling ship, and mingling as it did with that of our foes, made a most hideous noise. By-and-by I heard the shot strike the sides of our ship; the whole scene grew

indescribably confused and horrible; it was like some awfully tremendous thunderstorm whose deafening roar is attended by incessant streaks of lightning, carrying death in every flash, and strewing the ground with the victims of the wrath; only, in our case, the scene was rendered more horrible than that by the presence of torrents of blood which dyed our decks.

The cries of the wounded now rang through all parts of the ship. These were carried to the cockpit as fast as they fell, while those more fortunate who were killed outright were immediately thrown overboard. As I was stationed but a short distance from the main hatchway, I could catch a glance at all who were carried below. A glance was all that I could indulge in, for the boys belonging to the gun next to mine were wounded in the early part of the action, and I had to spring with all my might to keep three or four guns supplied with cartridges. I saw two of these lads fall nearly together. One of them was struck in the leg by a large shot; he had to suffer amputation above the wound. The other had a grape canister shot sent through his ankle. A stout Yorkshireman lifted him in his arms, and hurried him to the cockpit. He had his foot cut off, and thus was made lame for life. Two of the boys stationed in the quarterdeck were killed. They were both Portuges. A man who saw one of them killed, afterwards told me that his powder caught fire and burnt the flesh almost off his face. In this pitiable situation, the agonised boy lifted up both hands, as if imploring relief, when a passing shot instantly cut him in two . . .

I also observed a boy named Cooper, stationed at a gun some distance from the magazine. He came to and fro on the full run and appeared to be 'as merry as a cricket'. The third lieutenant cheered him always, occasionally by saying, 'Well done, my boy, you are worth your weight in gold.'

The fearful instance of burning described above was all too common; gunpowder was easily ignited by flying sparks, red-hot shot or the flash-back from gun breeches. To the modern mind it is extraordinary that these mere children – there were some on board even younger than Leech – surrounded by the sights and sounds of the bloody shambles that was a man-of-war's gundeck during an action, and with a good chance of being dreadfully hurt themselves, did not simply run away and hide. Leech offers an explanation, in retrospect thirty years on:

I have often been asked what were my feelings during this fight. I felt pretty much as I suppose everyone does at such a time. We all appeared cheerful, but I know that many a serious thought ran through my mind; still, what could we do at least but keep up a semblance of animation? To run from our quarters would have been certain death at the hands of our officers; to give way to gloom, or to show fear, would do no good, and might brand us with the name of cowards, and ensure certain defeat. Our only true philosophy therefore, was to make the best of a situation, by fighting bravely and cheerfully. I thought a great deal, however, of the other world; every groan, every falling man, told me that at the next instant I might be before the judge of all the earth. For this, I felt unprepared; but being without any particular knowledge of religious truth, I satisfied myself by repeating again and again the Lord's Prayer, and promising that if spared I would be more attentive to religious duties than ever before.[6]

Charles M'Pherson, a seaman in the *Genoa* in Admiral Sir Edward Codrington's combined fleet at the Battle of Navarino in 1827, describes another incident involving boys caught in a gun-action. Embellished as it is with the somewhat florid sentimentality of the age, his account is harrowing enough:

About half an hour after the action had commenced, two boys, of the names of Fisher and Anderson, the one about 14 years of age, the other about 12, both servants to the officers in the wardroom, were standing on the after hatch-way gratings, nearly abreast of the gun I was quartered at, on the lower deck. They were both fine-looking boys and neatly dressed in jacket and trousers. Fisher indeed, was the most interesting boy I ever saw. His cheeks were blooming with health and his large black eyes were shaded with long black curled hair. They were standing, as I said, on the gratings, hand-in-hand, and raising their tiny voices amidst the cheers of our men. I was loading the gun, and, not a moment before, had cried upon Fisher to go to the fore magazine for some tubes, when a shrill shriek sounded in my ears, and turning round, I saw Fisher lying a lifeless corpse. Anderson had also fell wounded, but not mortally; his right leg was nearly cut across, and one of his arms was hurt in several places. But it was not himself he cared for. He crawled to the corpse of Fisher, and burying his head in his dead companion's bosom, uttered the most piercing cries I have ever heard.

Another and I were ordered to take him to the cockpit. We found Fisher had been struck by a shot in the back of the head. A smile was on his lips, and his cheeks were ruddy as ever. It was with great difficulty that we could separate little Anderson from the body of his comrade. He implored us not to take his 'dear Ned' from him. Surrounded as we were with death and danger, it was impossible not to be affected at this scene; but we were obliged to use force and tear him away. The poor boy's sufferings were not complete; for as he was being taken to the cockpit, a splinter struck his right arm and broke it. Fisher was laid down among the common heap of slain, to await a watery grave.[7]

There were doubtless many earlier instances of the slaying and maiming of juveniles which are not recorded, as it is only from the late eighteenth century that the lower deck experience is handed down to us in the memoirs and journals of common seamen. Navarino, fought in October 1827, was the last major sea battle of the wooden-wall era, and we hear no more of mutilated adolescents until the Battle of Jutland gave the nation another boy-hero in the person of Jackie Cornwell of HMS *Chester*, awarded a posthumous Victoria Cross for remaining at his post though mortally wounded. He was one of eight Boy Seamen slain in *Chester* alone, out of a complement of fifteen. But it is only to modern eyes that there is anything remarkable in the spectacle of boys of such tender years as Leech and Anderson being exposed to violent death or injury in battle. The boys themselves took it for granted, as their reminiscences make clear; and so did their adult shipmates, for they were full members of the ship's company and had their part to play in fighting the ship. (Boys received their share of any prize money awarded for an enemy ship captured and taken into port. Prize money was paid out after the First World War, to the tune of £14,000,000, apportioned to the Navy as a whole. Admirals received £4,000, Boys £15). That part confined them to the duties of 'powder-monkey' only because they lacked the brawn to manhandle the great guns.

Not all men-of-war's boys were volunteers. Though a ten-year-old was safe from the press-gang, any much older were not. One such was Samuel Stokes, first pressed in 1806 when aged fourteen. Apprenticed to a baker in his home town of Ipswich, he had run away and shipped on a vessel in the coasting trade. On a voyage from the Thames estuary to Liverpool they ran foul of a French privateer off Land's End. Samuel escaped with some of the crew in the ship's boat and eventually reached Waterford on the south-east coast of Ireland. After many adventures, including a spell aboard the Press tender based at Waterford, where attempts were made to persuade him to volunteer, he contrived to get to Liverpool and took passage with a friendly captain for his home at Ipswich. Being warned by other vessels of much privateer presence up-Channel, they made towards Spithead with the intention of joining a convoy for the rest of the passage, under the protection of a man-of-war. Here was the seafarer's eternal dilemma when the press-gang was active: caught between the devil and the deep, privateer or press-gang. As they neared the great naval anchorage a frigate approached them. Samuel wanted to hide himself below, but the master assured him they would not take anyone so young. They did take him, and only him:

I was pressed and taken on board His Majesty's Brig the 'Richmond' May 13th 1806. My face is again turn'd from home, and my parents are disappointed of seeing me so soon as they expected, for I am going now to Gibraltar without any prospect of knowing whither, when, or ever I may reach home. Our passage was very short to Gibraltar. We laid here but a very short time before we was sent to cruise off the coast of Spain under the command of Admiral Harvey who was cruising off Cape Finisterre with six sail of the line, and he sent us to cruise off Vigo to blockade a Spanish privateer that was riding in that harbour. We had not been cruising many days, before our Captain received a letter from some person who was living at Vigo. The letter contained a full description of the privateer and his intention of coming out to take us. The hands was turned up and the letter read to the ship's company. I think it was about seven or eight days after, on the 7th of June in the morning as we lay to off the harbour's mouth, we see the privateer get under weigh and proceed to sea. Accordingly we made preparations for what we expected might be the event. The privateer having a superior number of men, he intended to run alongside and board us. We expected this to be his plan, as we had watched his motions very close and while he was in the act of shearing alongside, we gave him a broadside, and knocked away his foremast, and while he lay confused in this disabled state we sent our shot into him so fast, the proud Spaniard haul'd his colours down in sight of his own harbour and very probable in sight of some of their homes. Their loss was very great, ours was very little compar'd with theirs. As soon as we had cleared the deck and secured the guns, we took our prize in tow, and the next day in the afternoon we joined the Admiral, and the prisoners were sent ashore with a flag of truce two or three days after, and we went to Gibraltar to refit. We was near a month at Gibraltar this time, and then was sent to cruise on the coast of Spain . . . we chased a large American ship into Lisbon. She was loaded with a Spanish cargo. Lisbon being a neutral port at this time, he was safe as soon as he got over the bar. Nevertheless we went into Lisbon too, and lay there until the ship came out again, and a very few hours after she sailed we followed her out, and the same afternoon we made a prize of her, and sent her into England.

Little to choose here between man-of-war and privateer: one man's terrorist is another's freedom-fighter. No doubt the American was a blockade-runner, but it was such cavalier treatment of her ships which led to the war of 1812 with the United States. This capture would have yielded much prize-money for Samuel's ship but he was not to receive his share for he had 'run' before it was paid out. He had never reconciled himself to the king's service, and looked for an opportunity to desert. The opportunity came when he contrived, with desertion in mind, to be chosen as crew of the captain's gig. He patiently bided his time until:

On 27th May we sail'd from Cork to Portsmouth to refit, and arrived at Portsmouth the 3rd of June 1807, and on 15th June, after putting the Captain ashore at sallyport he gave me leave to stop ashore until the next day. I slept in Portsmouth that night, but my mind was very much agitated all night what I had best do. I was very much inclined to run away, but the dread of being punished if I did not get clear without being stopt almost deter'd me from making the attempt, and the thought of returning was a torment to me. Therefore I determined on making my escape whatever might be the event. Accordingly I rose very early in the morning and got safely out of Portsmouth before the sun rose. I was obliged to be cautious not to travel through any town I could possibly avoid, as the soldiers at that time would stop all travellers that had the appearance of sailors. On the third day after I left Portsmouth I got to London and went to Mill Stairs where the Ipswich corn vessels generally lay at that time. I found several there. I went on board the 'Griffin' and told the master my case. He offered me some refreshment which I readily accepted as I had not eat anything since the night before I left Portsmouth.

This fifteen-year-old boy must have been fainting with hunger after three days without a bite of food. But even that would not have driven him to revealing himself to the coasting skipper if he had feared being turned in for the sake of the bounty paid for capture of run seamen. Having sailed in a merchantman himself, he would know how much the press-gang was hated in the merchant service, the most fruitful source of crews for the king's ships in times of war, which was most of the time. His trust was not misplaced:

The following day I left London in the 'Daisy' a small vessel bound to Ipswich. Now I thought I was quite out of danger, but when we got down to the Nore, we found the man-of-war's boats was pressing very sharp. This a little surprised me and I was obliged to stow myself away in the hold with two others that had run away as well as myself and we pass'd through the fleet unnoticed or at least without being stopt. We had now only to fear being boarded going in Harwich, but Providence smiled on me to the end and the same night we got into Ipswich river. And the next tide we got up to Ipswich quay and I went home quite unexpected on the 12th of June to the joy of my parents. For they had not heard from me but once since I was press'd.[8]

With Bonaparte at last and finally borne away in HMS *Northumberland* to exile and death on St Helena, vast numbers of the king's ships were paid off and the loathed press-gangs disbanded, though the legal power of impressment was held in reserve (it remains on the statute books to this day). The effective ending of the press-gang meant that the Royal Navy became almost a volunteer service, much reduced in size as it was. Almost – because one source of recruitment was emphatically not voluntary: that of convicted smugglers. With the high duties imposed on luxury goods such as tea, tobacco, brandy and silks to pay for the war, and their scarcity because of it (many smugglers colluded with the French enemy to run contraband through the blockade), smuggling was a booming business at this date. With the end of the war, many more Navy ships were made available to assist the hard-pressed revenue men in their work, and increasing numbers of smugglers were brought to book. They were without exception superb seamen, and the Admiralty conveyed their view to magistrates that such men were wasted as gaol-fodder. The smugglers for the most part, had they been asked, would have preferred prison to service in a man-of-war, but they were not consulted and many hundreds were drafted to the Fleet.

With the coming of peace impressment could no longer be justified and, indeed, would not have been tolerated. The wholesale paying-off of ships during the first three years of peace, however, had meant a staggering reduction in naval manpower from a peak of 145,000 to a mere 19,000; barely enough for the Navy's peacetime requirements. This situation brought forcefully to the Admiralty's notice the disadvantages of their time-honoured method of manning ships, and they began to consider some form of 'continuous service' for seamen. Obvious candidates to form the core of a 'volunteer' Navy were the boys. When men-of-war were paid off the seamen gratefully resumed, like men returned from the dead, their former existences. Most boys, on the other hand, had known no other life, having been 'bred to the Navy'; besides, many were orphans or waifs and had nowhere else to go. The Navy, in its charity, did not turn them loose to beg and steal for a living; boys from decommissioned ships were found berths elsewhere while their Lordships considered ways and means of introducing, gradually at first, a system of long-term engagements for seamen.

In 1835 a newly-formed Manning Committee decreed that all Boy Seamen on reaching the age of eighteen were to be signed-on for ten years. This revolutionary measure[9] was, within a decade, to be extended to all ratings. Thereafter, when a ship decommissioned, its crew were drafted to other, active, ships in the Fleet, repeatedly up to the man's discharge at the end of his engagement: this was what was meant by 'continuous service'. On completion of his first ten-year engagement the erstwhile boy whose character and efficiency were good could sign up for a second ten years and take his discharge, with a pension, at the age of thirty-eight. This was a considerable inducement.

The second category to be embodied in the 'new' Navy were the Seamen Gunners. This was about the only specialism open to the old-time seaman, and it carried extra pay of threepence per day, so the Seamen Gunners had more of an incentive to make a career in the Navy. But the war of 1812 had shown up deficiencies in British naval gunnery: the Nelsonian dictum of 'engage the enemy more closely', which had served so well against the French, was less effective against the skilful gunnery of the United States frigates. In 1830 HMS *Excellent* was established at Portsmouth as a gunnery school. Such an institution had been advocated for years by scientifically-minded officers with an enthusiasm for gunnery. The following passage comes from a naval journal of 1832:

Their Lordships have directed that a certain number of active and carefully chosen seamen, not above thirty years of age shall be engaged for five years at an advanced rate of pay, and at the expiration of this period, the term may be renewed, at a further advance of pay. From this body of men, duly instructed, it is proposed that, in future, the gunners, gunners' mates and yeomen of the powder-room, will be selected, in order that they may communicate to the whole crew of the ships to which they may be appointed, the knowledge which they have acquired at the depot.

This combination of an enhanced rate of pay, pride in being, by contemporary standards, highly trained specialists and a real chance of advancement to warrant rank, meant that there was no shortage of volunteers. Henceforth these two groups, the Boy Seamen and the Seaman Gunners, formed the nucleus of the 'new' Royal Navy as the Victorian age dawned. Though it was to be another twenty years before continuous service was universal throughout the Fleet, for the first time the Navy was a service in which a boy could look ahead to a structured career.

TWO

Boys in the Victorian Navy

We arrived at Portland the next day and then I was transferred to the *Boscawen*. She was to be my home for 12 months and I arrived on board on November 14th 1870.

I cannot describe those 12 months of learning discipline. We were very often short of food and many a rope's end did I feel. Our instructors were very cruel, but I suppose it was mainly because we had a very stern captain. Life in the Navy was not thought much of. Our instruction comprised: Sail drill, knots and splices, boat rowing, gun drill, rifle and cutlass drills and everything that goes to make a sailor. We were taught to make and mend our own clothes and to wash them every Thursday. That day was known as 'Ropeyarn Sunday'. We were paid the large sum of threepence per week and if we liked and if our characters admitted, we were allowed to go ashore for a run every afternoon until sunset. At midsummer those who had homes and whose parents could afford it, were allowed to go home for three weeks. Those who stayed behind had to clean the ship and do other work, but no drills took place during the holidays. The same thing happened at Christmas. Being a long way from home and my parents very poor, I had to remain on board. This seemed very hard when I saw other boys go on leave and enjoy themselves. . . .[1]

From the mid-nineteenth century onwards, Boy Seamen's reminiscences are almost exclusively of their lives and hard times in the training ships. Many of them are quoted in the pages which follow: the most striking thing about them is their similarity. Decades pass, a new century dawns, revolutionary changes take place in the Navy's ships and weapons, and yet these divers accounts cannot be dated by their content alone, for nothing changes. In Boy Humphreys' recollections above, substitute 'Physical training' for 'Sail drill' and you have the Boy Seaman training curriculum of eighty years later. Eighty years later, a boy's pay had increased ten-fold to two shillings and sixpence per week (12½p), but so had the price of postage stamps and tooth-powder, and there was certainly no daily 'run ashore'.

Following the introduction of continuous service in an attempt to solve the problem of manning the Fleet, the Admiralty appointed HMS *Illustrious* as its first training ship for boys in 1854. It was hoped to inculcate in them a love of the sea and pride in the Queen's service. The experiment was a success, so much so that soon afterwards a similar scheme was introduced for naval cadets, whose education and training hitherto had left much to be desired. More training ships were commissioned, all of them square-rigger sailing ships, in the face of some opposition from progressively minded senior officers who opposed sail-training for the Navy as sail was increasingly replaced by steam. Their case was strengthened by a public outcry over the sinking of two training ships with great loss of life. The frigate *Eurydice* foundered in a squall off Sandown Bay in 1878, and two years later the *Atalanta* was lost on her homeward voyage from Bermuda. A total of 310 trainees drowned, in addition to the ships' companies. Sail-training continued to the very end of the century, despite the fact that sail had all but disappeared in the Fleet twenty years earlier.

As sailing ships were paid off and decommissioned, most went to the breaker's yard; a few, stripped of most of their sails and rigging, were moored in the vicinity of naval ports to accommodate boys under training – the thoroughly detested 'hulks'. To each was attached a sailing-brig to provide the required sea-going experience. The hulks provided the initiation and basic training of boy entrants, and by 1870 there were three: at Falmouth, Portland and Portsmouth. A spell of 'deep-sea' training in sail followed the year or so spent in the training ships. In the ensuing pages we hear the authentic voices of these boys, recording the minutiae of their daily lives. I 'interrupt' their accounts where a particularly apposite parallel can be drawn with the regime, described in another chapter, in HMS *Ganges*, the principal boys' training establishment some seventy years later. First, Thomas Holman describes the routine in HMS *St Vincent* at Portsmouth in 1872:

At 5.30 a.m. in summer the reveille would sound on all decks on which the boys slept; this was followed first by the shrill notes of the Bosun's Mates' pipes, and then by three deep bass voices . . . 'Now, rouse out, rouse out, show a leg'. Once out, the next thing was to lash up one's hammock, as quickly and neatly as possible, and hurry on deck. The next duty was to scrub and wash the decks (on Saturday holystone them); this was generally finished by 6.30 when all the boys that could swim were allowed to bathe overboard . . . how late we often used to be for breakfast which was begun at quarter to seven, and finished at 7.15. Half the boys then had to dress for going on deck; in summer time in white clothes, and white they must be, or woe betide the lad that was dirty. The other half, who remained below, cleaned out the messes and scrubbed the messdeck. At 8 o'clock there was what was known as 'morning evolution' which meant, for the most part, drill aloft in loosing and furling sails, and crossing the upper yards.

The evolution finished, at 9 a.m. the bugles sounded the 'assembly' and all the boys fell in, in rows, on the upper deck for inspection. The Instructors each had a section of twenty to thirty boys to look after, clothe and keep clean; four of these sections composed a division, to which was attached an officer for inspection and supervision. After most close scrutiny by the Instructor and officer, in which a dirty boy was soon spotted and warned, or, if necessary, awarded some minor punishment, the boys were all marched to the quarterdeck, and prayers read by the Chaplain or Captain. This over, the boys were 'told off' and immediately proceeded to instruction – one half going to school, and the other to seamanship and gunnery instruction.[2]

Seventy-five years on, in HMS *Ganges*, boys under training were similarly organized into classes and divisions and the morning routine was virtually identical, save for taking place in a shore barracks rather than a training-hulk. Boys went to 'cleaning stations' after breakfast, then changed into 'rig of the day' to be closely inspected by instructors and divisional officers. Classes were marched to the parade ground, where the chaplain led prayers before boys dispersed to training classes. In 1872,

> The seamanship instruction consisted of swimming, boat pulling, knots and splices, monkey topsail yard – i.e., a yard close to the deck on which the youngsters were taught to get in and out, and loose and furl sails, before they were allowed aloft – then bends and hitches, and, as a boy advanced, all the hull and rigging of a ship, compass, helm, lead etc. The gunnery consisted of working the guns, and rifle, and cutlass drill.

Swimming in 1947 came under physical training rather than seamanship, and, of course, sail training had long gone. Otherwise the curriculum was the same: knots and splices, bends and hitches, boxing the compass, helmsman's duties and hand lead-line. For this last, the training establishment at Shotley had erected on the foreshore a tall wooden tower rather like the guard-towers in prisoner-of-war camps and Alabaman penitentiaries. The lead was a six-pound sinker moulded on to an iron shank to which the lead-line was spliced; fifteen fathoms of light line with fathom markers along its length – a bit of cod-line with a knot in it, a bit of cod-line with two knots in it, a scrap of leather, a scrap of leather with a notch in it, and so on. These marks had to be learned by heart so that they were known – literally – blindfold, as soundings might be taken in darkness. The tall tower simulated the bows of a battleship, where the 'chains' were located: this was a small, vertiginous wooden platform projecting over the ship's bow where the leadsman stood. There was skill in swinging the lead (an etymologist might be able to tell us whence came the malingering connotation); the line was coiled in a special way to avoid snagging and held in the leadsman's left hand while the lead was lowered almost to the water and swung like a pendulum in ever-increasing arcs until, when almost horizontal, a well-judged tug on the line whirled the lead skywards to describe a sweeping circle. An ill-judged tug could garotte the leadsman. As the lead, with this impetus, swung again to the horizontal it was released, to splash into the sea ahead of a slowly moving ship (or on *Ganges'* foreshore, a

much-pitted patch of sand) to give the lead time to sink to the
bottom and sounding to be taken with the line straight up and
down as the ship passed over that spot. Well into the 1950s, with
all warships long before equipped with electronic echo-sounding
gear, a leadsman was always stationed in the chains of a ship
approaching harbour, presumably on the belt-and-braces
principle. Certainly hand lead-line was considered an important
subject in the postwar *Ganges* seamanship final examinations.
Thomas Holman continues:

> The brightest lads were always selected for instruction in
> signalling also; but this was a shame, for in those days the
> signalmen, although the most intelligent men in the fleet, had
> much the smallest field of promotion. It is different now, but
> not as good as it ought to be.

Not so different – seventy years later the brightest new entrants
were urged to opt for the Signals Branch, but some of them were
bright enough to realize, even then, that promotion prospects
were limited, with many fewer chief and petty officers than the
much bigger Seaman Branch.

> At 11.30 a.m. the instructions ceased, and the decks were
> again swept up for dinner. A number of the boys called 'cooks
> of the messes' together with the 'caterer' went below, fetched
> the food from the 'galley' where it was cooked, and allotted it
> out in plates – one for each boy in the mess. A basin of fairly
> nourishing soup, not less than half a pound of cooked meat,
> three or four potatoes and one half of a loaf, or a large slice of
> plum pudding, was the usual fare. One day each week we had
> pea soup and boiled pork. This was certainly not a bad dietary
> for a lad of fifteen to seventeen.

It certainly was not a bad diet, and a great deal better than his
successors enjoyed (see Chapter 4).

> The oldest boys always somehow contrived to receive the
> largest shares. At 12 o'clock, when all was ready, the bell
> struck eight and the bosun's mate piped to dinner, and every

boy rushed below to see what the plates contained. The first there stood up beside the plate that looked to him to contain the largest share. Then the bugle sounded 'The still'[3] and an officer passed around the messdeck to see if there was any complaint; and the caterer at the end of each table said grace as he passed. If a boy wished to complain, he stood at the end of his table, plate in hand, and invited the officer's attention to either the quantity, or the quality, as the case might be, of the food. The officer usually got out of any difficulties of this sort by calling for the plate of the boy who had portioned it out, and exchanging it for the one complained of. This was a healthy check on unfairness, and kept things pretty level. When the officer had gone round, he ordered 'carry on' to be sounded, and we fell to.

This dinner-time routine was pretty much the same in the mid-twentieth century. Boys were fallen-in clear of the messdeck while the food was dished out by the duty 'cooks of the mess'; when allowed in, a certain amount of jostling took place for the microscopically bigger portions, real or imagined. The cooks were already stood to the table, and if a vigilant instructor noticed that their portions were bigger than the rest, he would order everyone to move one place to the right (or sometimes to the left, to fox the cook who was cunning as well as greedy). No officer would be present on the messdeck to receive complaints or hear grace; in the modern wardroom, this would be pink-gin time. Instead, the instructor delivered himself of a purely ritualistic: 'Any complaints say grace', and we all gabbled 'For what we are about to receive may the Lord make us truly thankful', just as our forerunners did seventy years before, though with even less sincerity, as the food in 1947 was generally disgusting.

At one o'clock the 'assembly' sounded again, and we all fell in on the upper deck; and, if any boy was to be punished, we were all marched aft and saw the culprit, mounted on another boy's back, receive the number of strokes (from a cane) allotted him.

This seems unnecessarily cruel, for the unfortunate boy under sentence could hardly have relished his dinner with a thrashing in prospect immediately after. In the more enlightened 1940s, 'cuts' were always inflicted in the forenoon, so the victim could at least enjoy his dinner, albeit from a standing position.

From this we went to instruction again, the watch that had been to school in the morning going to seamanship and gunnery, and the other watch to school. At 3.30 the instruction again ceased, and, if washing night, we were ordered to put on blue clothing and bring our whites up. Washing tubs, ready filled with water, were placed along the deck, and the boys arranged on either side of them, four or six to each tub; the bugle sounded, and we each made a rush to the nearest tub and began to lather up. Instructors usually came to the assistance of the newly joined. At 5 o'clock we went to tea, and at 5.30 hung up our clothes to dry, on lines provided for the purpose. We next washed down the upper deck, and the remainder of the evening was our own.

This spartan, cold-water washday must have been a bleak ordeal in winter. The anonymous boy quoted on page 43 eulogizes the brand-new Shotley Barracks in 1905: 'You had dormitories, beds; you had a laundry . . .' That same laundry was in use in 1947; it resembled the old Peabody Buildings type of public wash-house, with rows of big, deep, glazed earthenware sinks flanked by slimy wooden scrubbing-boards. There were duck-boards on the cement floor and clothes were dried in a vast heated cabinet with a row of tall, narrow racks which slid out on rollers in a blast of hot air, to allow garments to be draped on the rails within. By then, there was no time set aside for washing clothes; it was done in the boys' own time, following a single session in the new entrant class when an instructor demonstrated the laundering of underwear, towels, jerseys and blue-jean collars. The importance of thorough rinsing was stressed, to avoid an affliction called 'dhobi itch', unknown outside the Navy and caused probably by the coarse, acerbic yellow soap used for washing both clothes and bodies. It was issued in crude, heavy bars like iron ingots and was known as 'pusser's hard'.

At eight o'clock the hammocks were 'piped down' and hung up ready for 'turning in'; and at 8.30 the decks were finally cleared up for the day. At 9.0 p.m. all lights were extinguished and every boy had to be in his hammock. The first Lieutenant then 'went the rounds' to see all correct for the night. After this silence should prevail, but seldom did, as the liveliest among us generally had a good story to tell, which would set all the others laughing, and this sometimes led to a whole tier, or row, of boys having to turn out, lash up their hammocks, and stand with them on their shoulders on the quarterdeck. This usually cooled both our heels and our ardour, and we were glad to go to sleep when allowed below again.

Officer's rounds were only carried out in the modern *Ganges* in the new entrant annexe to the main establishment, when, after 'Lights out', a small procession heralded by the shrill pipe of a bosun's call sounding the 'Still' and led by a quartermaster in a long, deep-collared watch-coat, carrying a large black lantern with a lighted candle in it, entered the dormitory. Next came the officer of the day, usually a commissioned gunner or boatswain, sometimes in evening dress of monkey-jacket, boiled shirt and black tie, with a glittering Royal Marine ship's police corporal bringing up the rear. This little cortege strode wordlessly to the end of the dormitory, wheeled about and marched to the door, the Nelsonian ship's lantern casting dramatic shadows on the walls. It is likely that this fleeting but romantic spectacle was intended to impress the highly impressionable 'nozzers', as new entrants were known. In *Ganges* proper, boys were 'piped down' by the duty instructor; officers in general were much less involved in the boys' daily lives than had been their Victorian counterparts. There was a similar, but harsher, traditional punishment for dormitories talking after 'Pipe down' (see Chapter 4).

Reflecting in later years on the indiscriminate cruelty inflicted on boys, Holman writes:

I remember the first time I became acquainted with this same cane was by a cut at random from one of the ship's police, who, out of pure fun or devilment, was dealing out in the most liberal way, slashes, both right and left, to any of us poor hapless youngsters who happened to be in the sphere of his operations.

This state of affairs existed twenty years ago, and, I have no hesitation in saying, it was a scandal and disgrace to the authorities that such men as those Ship's Police and Petty Officers – the majority of whom was then largely, or totally, uneducated, and with no sense of judicial fairness, should be free to wreak their own sweet will on the boys, who were without a chance of appeal or redress, placed under their care. Those days are however gone, relegated to the limbo of the past, and today we are verging on the other extreme; for so rigid are the regulations, that should any of the instructors on board our training ships strike a boy, even under aggravating circumstances, he is at once reduced from a Petty Officer to an Able Seaman, and sent out of the Training Service. This is placing dangerous power in the hands of the boys, who are sometimes not above using it in combining to ruin a Petty Officer; still it is, in my opinion, the lesser evil of the two, and the Instructors are certainly much more able to look after themselves now than we boys were then.

Holman made the above observation in 1892, and claims that by that date no instructor would dare lay a finger on a boy. Odd, then, that both Austin and Minchin (see Chapter 3) complain of physical violence on the part of instructors in 1898 and 1906 respectively. Holman, it seems certain, had an exaggerated idea of the extent to which things had changed since his day, in common with other 'old salts' who voice their opinions about this time. Certainly, in the post-war, atomic-age HMS *Ganges* instances of instructors striking boys, though perhaps not everyday occurrences, were common enough. It was not, of course, officially condoned, though the few instructors given to the practice took little trouble to conceal it; as, for instance, in the case of the class being marched across the parade ground in broad daylight, with the instructor beating out the step with the back of his hand on an inattentive boy's ear. Other cases are cited in a later chapter.

H.J. Austin, a boy aboard the original HMS *Ganges*, a hulk moored off Falmouth in 1898, remembers:

Monday morning was always sail drill. Thursday morning was always inspection day. One half had their clothing laid out for inspection and the other half their hammocks and bedding laid out, changing round weekly. Thursday was always make and mend afternoon, when most boys looked over their clothing or wrote letters and the bumboat came. Friday was all day instruction but Saturday was clean ship. The watch on deck holystoning the deck from 9 till 11 a.m. After stand easy it was a case of washing down and drying up the decks with swabs till dinner time. The watch below were busy scrubbing mess tables and stools, then the deck, after which deck cloths were put down and the Instructors went round and inspected the messes to find out if any knives, forks or spoons or anything was missing, ready for the Officer's inspection.[4]

In the 1947 *Ganges*, boys laid out their kit for inspection on alternate Wednesdays; one class mustering kits, the other going to school for the forenoon. Every item was laid out on the made-up bed in the regulation fashion illustrated by a diagram in the *Admiralty Manual of Seamanship* Volume I, issued to every boy on joining. Each piece of clothing was folded in a particular way and then rolled into a tight cylinder of precisely identical width, with the owner's name uppermost. The uniformity of width was achieved by using that same *Seamanship Manual* as a gauge. Thus, the hem of every garment – jumper, jersey, trousers, flannel vests, underpants – was placed between its pages before folding and rolling. The 'swiss roll' so achieved was held together by 'clothes-stops', short lengths of cod-line tied with a neat reef knot and the ends tucked under, and laid out in the prescribed place. It took more than one pair of hands so a boy was assisted by his neighbour, who was assisted in return. It also took a long time, most of the morning. When all was finished, kits were inspected first by the class instructor and then by the divisional officer; the latter with great thoroughness, always wearing kid gloves and fastidiously pulling off clothes-stops and shaking out the garment, holding it at arm's length and letting it fall in a heap on the bed. Clothing could have been just as effectively inspected for cleanliness and good repair had the garments been neatly folded and laid-out, and it would have been a good deal easier and quicker. This, presumably, disqualified such a method, and no doubt explained why extra dogwatch kit musters were frequently awarded as punishment. Boy Austin was fortunate, no make and mend afternoon was allotted at Shotley, though HM ships usually enjoyed one a week at the commander's discretion; 'a make-and-mend' was Navalese for an afternoon off, and was generally spent in sleeping after the rum issue.

In 1947, Saturday mornings were spent in scrubbing-out messes for captain's rounds. Mess tables and stools were hauled outside and scrubbed in the open air, with cold water and the previously mentioned pusser's hard, while decks within were scrubbed or polished as appropriate; wash-room and lavatories ('heads') scrubbed and brass fittings polished with 'Bluebell' and cotton-waste to a blinding gleam, all done under the chivvying of instructors increasingly anxious as the time for rounds approached. At last, with furniture replaced and sparkling 'mess-traps' laid out, the boys, grubby and dishevelled from their labours, were told to 'lose' themselves; retiring in summer to the foreshore, or in winter to the 'day heads', brick-built blocks behind the messes where an added attraction was a large coke-burning brazier placed there in the coldest weather to prevent the plumbing freezing up. The progress of rounds from mess to mess was signalled by the sound of the Marine bugler's 'Still' as he led the procession. Next came the Captain, followed as always by the Commander, then the Master-at-Arms and finally, the Royal Marine Colour Sergeant resplendent in red sash and white cotton gloves. An apprehensive Divisional Officer reported the mess correct to the Captain, who returned his salute and entered the mess, followed by his retinue. Inspection was thorough. The Commander was very tall, and from his great height could see things that the Captain, who was very short, could not; from time to time he would beckon the Marine sergeant forward to run a white-gloved finger along a ledge, and if it came away soiled there was trouble. Where more than one or two such oversights were detected, the unfortunate mess was ordered a 're-scrub' on Saturday afternoon.

Sunday was, of course, the best day. The reveille at quarter past six – long after the sun had started to peek through the portholes. How we used to enjoy that extra forty-five minutes in our hammocks! Then there was no cleaning decks; simply to bathe and breakfast. After breakfast we dressed in our very best and cleanest to go to decks; a few only remaining below to clean up 'tween decks. 'Divisions' was at 9.30 on Sunday and the Captain used always to come around and inspect both the boys and the ship. I was on these occasions the most envied of boys, for he would occasionally ask me how I was getting on, and if I liked it. After Divisions, Church; which I must confess was the first divine service I ever cared for – there seemed a dash of romance in it. Church was followed by the best dinner of the week, and this again by a run on shore for those who wished, a few only being compelled to stay, and these only for the purpose of pulling the rest on shore, or in case of fire on the ship. We used to land at 1.30, and come off at 6.30. The evenings on Sunday were much the same as other evenings, except that we were not allowed aloft.

Post war Shotley Sundays began with reveille at 7 a.m. No early-morning cleaning was required after the exertions of Saturday, and breakfast was at 7.30. Sunday's was the best breakfast of the week – bacon and egg (one egg, one rasher) and butter for the bread instead of margarine. Breakfast was followed by a flurry of preparation for Sunday Divisions, the major parade of the week. The wiser souls had spent Saturday afternoon in preparing for it; queuing for a turn with the mess's one electric iron between forty-odd boys. Blue-jean collars were required to have three vertical creases; trousers, six horizontal ('athwartship') creases equidistant along each leg. Sunday Divisions was a lengthy affair; officers with swords and both officers and instructors a-jingle with medals as the band tootled and *parped* on a muted note its repertoire of Strauss and Gilbert and Sullivan while the Captain's entourage made its leisurely progress through all divisions. Then the march past and to Divine Service in the gymnasium. (*Ganges* possessed a chapel but it was very small and for some reason tucked away in a basement; it was used for communion services, baptisms and confirmation classes). After church, divisions marched back to dinner.

The rest of Sunday was the boys' own. Most spent it in reading and writing letters; in fine weather wandering the playing fields or foreshore. Games and mast-climbing were forbidden on the sabbath. A few Boys took advantage of the only 'shore-leave' permitted. This was known as 'Shotley leave' and was hardly worth the trouble. Boys were allowed out of the main gates to stretch their legs along five miles of rural road, with endless vistas of flat ploughland, cows and haystacks to refresh the weary spirit. The limit was defined by a crossroads and any boy caught beyond this point was assumed to have it in mind to 'do a bunk', and was dealt with accordingly. Any boy taking advantage of this liberty had to remain straitened in best uniform to be closely inspected by the officer of the day both on departure and return.

I think I have shown in the preceding pages that the only significant changes in the daily lives of boy seamen under training over a span of seventy years derive from two wholly economic/technical developments: the discontinuance of sail training at the end of the last century, and the transfer from training-hulks to shore barracks soon afterwards. Sweeping social and political changes in society at large during the first half of the twentieth century, plus two world wars, had had little or no influence on the British Admiralty's philosophy of indoctrination and training of its boy entrants; though change was soon to come.

After 1945, these attitudes were reinforced by the Navy's senior officer establishment's hankering, following six years of dilution by reserve officers and hostilities-only ratings, for a return to the pre-war status quo. The HMS *Ganges* which the author encountered in January 1947, described in some detail in later chapters, was a remarkable Victorian time-capsule embedded in the post-atomic Royal Navy. There is no doubt that the HMS *Ganges* of that time left its mark on a boy; nor that later, when he went to sea, being 'a Shotley boy' brought its advantages in regard to early responsibility and promotion prospects. Most of my contemporaries look back on their *Ganges* experience with retrospective pride as well as wonder. No change there, either, for Thomas Holman concludes:

Looking back on those days brings many pleasant reminiscences, from which I even now derive much pleasure.

We were well fed, and generally well cared for in body and mind; the schooling we received laid the foundation of a desire to seek after a knowledge that afterwards bore fruit in many ways advantageous to us and the service.

Likewise a near-contemporary of Holman's aboard *St Vincent*:

Altogether my days in the 'St Vincent' slid along as happy and full of events as any boy could wish. I was eighteen months aboard of her, and passed out of my classes creditably. The days were employed in instruction in everything that can make a man useful, the evenings in play or study, or writing home. I loved the life, there was a flavour and a tang about it as sweet as the sea itself. It was full of interest, full of adventure, full of possibility, full of change.[5]

THREE

The Dreadnoughts

The revolutionary *Dreadnought* was the culmination, brought together in one design, of three fundamental developments in warship construction since HMS *Victory*: wood replaced by iron and steel, sail by steam and broadside guns by revolving turrets firing armour-piercing shells. These changes had evolved over half a century; nevertheless *Dreadnought* was indeed revolutionary and not merely evolutionary, because her design represented a great technological advance. Her compact turbines, replacing space-wasting, inefficient reciprocating engines, gave her a cruiser's speed; she had thicker armour than any previous warship and her armament consisted of ten 12–inch guns mounted in pairs in turrets which were director-controlled, secondary armament being dispensed with. Her ship's company numbered upwards of a thousand; such a large complement, resulting in notoriously cramped living conditions, was a fighting necessity. Complements were determined, then and later, by the numbers required to man the guns, shell rooms, magazines and stokeholds in action – considerably more than the ironclads needed.

Of course, overcrowding was traditional in a warship's 'tween-decks. So were wooden walls, sail-power and muzzle-loading cannon. But these had been swept away; not so the seamen's broadside messes, the issuing of raw victuals for the men to prepare themselves, the 14 inches allotted to each man in which to sling his hammock – the sailor's best friend. No design expertise had been laid out on improving ventilation to fetid, condensation-dripping messdecks. British naval architects had, until recent times, no tradition of looking much to the human needs of lower deck ratings. A leading practitioner of the art some years ago confirmed what I had always suspected, that the elite Corps of Naval Constructors, on receiving a design order for, say, a new class of 6–inch cruiser, laid out the necessary machinery, guns and other armaments, magazines, shellrooms, fire-control systems, storage spaces and fuel tanks, all within the overall dimensions needed for the required speed and tonnage; then, almost as an afterthought, squeezed in some living-spaces among and between all these fighting essentials. Such was not the case in other modernized navies whose ships were efficient, superbly designed fighting machines, and yet provided their crews with decent, tolerably comfortable accommodation. A further long-established naval tradition reversed in the Dreadnoughts was the accommodating of officers forward and ratings aft, over the vibrating propellers.

From 1907 the Anglo–German naval race was on, and seven more Dreadnoughts were to be launched by the outbreak of hostilities in 1914, giving the Royal Navy a slender margin of superiority over the German High Seas Fleet. Meantime, many more seamen (and stokers) were needed to man these leviathans. Royal Naval manpower, of all ranks and ratings, increased from 60,000 in 1889 to 140,000 in 1913. As described in an earlier chapter, an important source of naval recruitment had for many years been philanthropic institutions like the Marine Society and others, such as the Royal Hospital School at Greenwich. This was a boarding school specifically for the sons of Royal Navy seamen, linked with Greenwich Hospital for naval in-pensioners. Entry to either establishment was by no means guaranteed, with the patronage of a senior officer usually necessary. This was gained on behalf of his young son by one John Bechervaise, a petty officer quartermaster of long and arduous service. He records a visit to the school in 1824:

We called at Greenwich to see our dear boy; it is really gratifying to the eye of a parent to see the cleanliness and comfort that pervades the place, they all looked cheerful and healthy; as for mine, who was but just ten years of age, a sweet chubby boy, had the glow of health and happiness on his cheek: how happy I felt while pressing him to my bosom and blessed the hand of those who had placed him in that happy institution. I begged permission to see the Captain now

Admiral McKinley who then had command; on his appearing, I begged leave to return my sincere and humble thanks, not only for the admission of the child, but for the care which had been taken of him. I got permission for him to come out for the evening and also to spend most of the next day with me, which was a great favour as it was the fair week when none of the boys were allowed out.[1]

Greenwich boys made up a significant proportion of the Navy's intake in mid-century, varying between 5 and 10 per cent. The Greenwich regime was strict and spartan, as all charitable boarding schools of the age were, but the young Bechervaise had apparently thrived there. The following description of the school dates from the closing years of Victoria's reign, by a Greenwich boy whose father was a coastguard:

In about 1904 there was another boy who came home from Greenwich School – his father lived not very far from us – and I used to admire him. I asked my father if I could wear the same uniform and he said he was a Greenwich School boy and asked me if I wanted to go to Greenwich School. I said I would like to go like that. My father said that he wouldn't send me, but that I had to use my own discretion. I was a bit fed up with having to walk three miles to school each day. My brother Fred told me that I wouldn't like it, but I told him that he was only jealous because he couldn't go there. My old dad took me up there; he knew I was fit because he used to join the boys for the Navy – that was part of his job – and he introduced me to the Chief Officer of Greenwich School, Mr Read. I think they knew one another and I also had two elder brothers in the Navy.

I went into No. 5 dormitory and my instructor was Mr Pallett. The school was absolutely Navy and very severe and strict. We had beds and there were 120 boys in my dormitory. Two of them were Petty Officer Boys, and they used to sleep in a bed on their own at either end of the room, and whatever you did they had their eye on you, and they carried these stonnachies and they had supreme control, and they weren't frightened to use the old stonnachies either. And if you did misbehave they could do anything them boys could. Young men they were, just about to go into the Service. Physically fit, good at gymnastics, good at everything and their education was good, otherwise they wouldn't have been made a Chief Petty Officer Boy. They put them in charge of us other boys. I got along all right, I got in a bit of a fight with another boy one day – you know what boys will be. If they don't like one another they will have a go. It lasted a good while this fight did but we were too small to really hurt one another and the instructor saw that you fought it out. 'We'll square the difference out between you', he said, 'don't matter how long it lasts.' After it was all over you shook hands and were friends for ever more. When I was fourteen I had to go and pass the sea test. I passed all right and then you went and lived aboard the ship that was in the parade ground, the 'Fame' for nine months so they prepared you for going to sea. She was the biggest model of a ship in the world. The boys built her themselves before my time.[2]

It was a hard life for young boys fresh from home, as boys' training always had been and would continue to be.

There were many times when I used to think to myself 'I wish to God I hadn't come', but I couldn't rebel because I'd gone off my own bat. I used to tell my father that everything was fine, but I wasn't allowed to take my uniform off on leave, as my father being Chief Officer in the Coastguard had a position to keep up. He had been promoted again and was now at West Mersey on Hayling Island; there were twenty-one Gobbies[3] there.[4]

This Greenwich schoolboy could not admit he was finding it hard, giving 'brother Fred' the chance to say 'I told you so!' The 120–bed dormitory must have acclimatized boys to living conditions afloat. Still, he had some good times:

Then they used to teach us hornpipe, roller skates, gymnastics, up the mast. Some of them would fight each other as to who would be Cap Boy – the boy who would climb up the mast and

stand on the top. I learnt a lot while I was there. I learnt to use
a sailmaker's needle, how to make a suit, how to use a sextant.
We used to make our own clothes in Greenwich – you'd have
so many weeks in the tailor's shop and so many in the
carpenter's shop – all the different trades.

You had a certain amount of free time. At 4 o'clock we'd
have our tea and you had a bit of bread and cheese at 8
o'clock and then you'd go to bed but from tea time until supper
time you'd be messing around with your bag or seeing to your
clothes. I played football and cricket for my company and once
I played cricket for the school. We had our cricket field round
at the back where the observatory is. I was a good little sailor
boy; I used to hope that the boat would turn over to see what
would happen! That was the sort of boy I was.[5]

This lad, as was traditional in the case of boy entrants, came of
a seafaring background, living on the coast with an ex-Royal
Navy father and serving brothers. With the great expansion
in recruitment at this time the naval-connection intake
was considerably diluted, with boys from homes with no naval
tradition. In these cases it was usually the son who chose
the Navy, not the parent. A father might be approving of his
son's choice, perhaps indifferent, sometimes strongly opposed –
and the latter case presented a difficulty, as parental permission
was required for a boy to enlist. The determined youngster
would persist:

At that time, unemployment was rife. I came from a little
market town, Bishop's Stortford, and there were tons of people
out of work and although I was only a youngster I thought it
was the best thing I could do to join the Navy. I had always
wanted to join the Service; I wanted to wear a sailor's collar
and be a Jolly Jack. My father at first wasn't going to sign but I
worried him so much that he gave way and said: 'If you go,
you make your own bed. It's no good wanting to come back!'

How often must that parental warning have echoed down the
years! For some the need to enlist was more pressing, as William
Prayle records. Prayle 'adjusted' his age to join as a trainee

stoker. He ended his naval career as a Stoker Petty Officer, winning a Distinguished Service Medal in 1915.

I joined the Navy because I was hungry. I used to pick up orange peel in the street and eat that – good old days they call them! My father was an old time sailor in the Navy and deserted my mother when we were kids. I was at Poplar Work House. All the family were there because my father deserted. I later worked at a hospital at Byfleet for £6 a year. When I asked the matron for more money she said the funds didn't run to it so I said I was leaving on Saturday. I only had the suit of clothes I was standing up in, another coat and waistcoat and a change of under-gear. So on Saturday I went as I thought to Waterloo Station. I didn't know my way about London, so I asked where the home for working boys in London was. They said it was in Chelsea; threepence on the bus. I got to the home and then met an old school mate and he got me a job at a butcher's at ten shillings a week. I stayed there until I joined the Navy.[6]

All boy seamen recruits were entered into one of the training hulks moored at, or close to, naval bases. At the turn of the century there were five: *St Vincent* at Portsmouth, *Impregnable* at Devonport, *Boscawen* at Portland, *Ganges* at Falmouth and *Caledonia* at Queensferry. What follows is the account of a boy entrant, H.J. Austin, who joined HMS *Ganges* in the winter of 1898. Once more, the reader will note how little had changed from experiences of forty years earlier, described in Chapter 2. This is perhaps unsurprising in a service noted for its conservatism; also, social and living standards in the nation at large had changed hardly more. What is remarkable, as a later chapter will reveal, is how very little had changed in the Royal Navy's treatment of its boy entrants, in large matters as well as in small, fifty years after that. But first to Boy Austin's account:

We arrived at Falmouth at about 4 p.m. just as it was getting dusk and a steam Pinnace took us to the ship in St Juste pool off Mylor, three miles from Falmouth, and as soon as we scrambled up the gangway we were met by several boys saying,

'Have you got any scran?' (food) and they eagerly grabbed any sandwiches or pasties we had left but made a hurried departure when the Crusher (Ship's Police) arrived. We were then turned over to a Petty Officer Instructor, Mr Allsop, a most kindly man, who told us what we could do and could not do. After a time we were all given about half a pint of cocoa with no sugar or milk and the top floating with grease.[7]

In the late 1940s this same 'pusser's kye' – thick, greasy and unsweetened – was still being issued to boys; usually on rising as a literal 'break-fast' and accompanied by two or three hard-tack biscuits.

We were then taken to the Orlop deck[8] where there were hammocks slung, and we told to turn in folding our clothes up and putting them in the upper part of the hammock to serve as a pillow. We all got into our hammocks somehow being helped and pushed by the Instructor. I got to sleep all right but some other boys had a bad night.

We were awakened by loud whistling (bosun's pipes) and shouts of 'Cooks!' and 'Hammock stowers!' This meant that the boys detailed as cooks and hammock stowers had to get up. Then at six o'clock more piping and shouts of 'Show a leg!' That meant up we all got out of our hammocks but somehow a couple fell out. The Instructor (Mr Allsop) who it appeared always had the new-comers or Nozzers as we were called, sent one boy to the galley with a kettle for some cocoa (again without sugar or milk) but a lot of greasy yellow fat floating on top. One boy was sent to the galley to get some water to wash up the basins and then take the water on to the upper deck to empty it down a chute that led over the side. When we returned we were all trooped on to the upper deck to wash in cold water in a tub. It was very cold and frosty. We were told to dry ourselves on our shirts, as we were being kitted up that day and would be given towels then. We were then instructed how to fold the blanket, (we all had one each), straighten the bed, and place the blanket on the bed ready for lashing up. Each hammock had to be neatly lashed with seven turns equidistant apart. We all had to lash and unlash several times before the Instructor was satisfied and by that time it was eight o'clock breakfast. . . .

If this account is accurate, these nozzers (a term still in use fifty years later, see Chapter 4) had taken two hours to rise, consume cocoa, wash and dress, lash-up and stow hammocks. Twenty minutes to half an hour would normally be allowed for this early-morning routine, in 1897 and 1947 alike, but new entrants were usually broken in gently, 'gently' being a relative term. A new-entrant instructor was selected from the older petty officers for his relative qualities of patience and humanity – Boy Austin describes his instructor as 'a most kindly man'.

Another boy was sent for the tea. This was made by the Chief Cook pouring water on the tea in a huge wooden tub. This would be ladled out according to the number in the mess. So our breakfast was tea, no milk and a very little sugar and a slice of dry bread, no butter, margarine or jam. This was always the breakfast, except that two days a week we were given a piece of fat boiled pork. It was well boiled, so we were able to spread it on the bread like lard. When the weather was too bad for the bread boat to come out to us we had a hard biscuit in place of the bread. At 8.30 clear up decks, 8.45 muster on the quarterdeck for Divisions. Turned aft to see the colours hoisted then Prayers. After Prayers, dismiss and all went to their places of instruction. We new boys were taken to be kitted up. We were given our kit and after you had got it all you went below with a type cut in wood; you marked all your clothes with your name in paint; white paint on blue, and black paint on the others. After this we were shown how to fold our clothes and tie them up with clothes stops.

Wooden types and black and white paint were still being used to mark newly-issued kit, exactly as described here, in HMS *Ganges* until 1960.

Dinner time came but just before twelve o'clock we were each given a card with Ship's Book Number on it, with Watch, part of Watch, No. of mess, name of Instructor. My instructor was

Mr Hooper a kind man. We were then shown our mess. I was
in No. 14 mess. Each mess had a Petty Officer Boy, or a boy
with a badge in charge, and these in turn had their own
bully boys. These boys detailed one of the boys to be cook of
the mess for a week and he was responsible for getting the
food when it was time and preparing it for cooking. This
usually meant washing the potatoes in salt water, putting
them in a large tin dish and putting the meat on top –
sometimes called 'Schooner on the Rocks' or if it was bony
called 'two spuds and a Jonah'.⁹ 10.30 am stand easy, a half
slice of dry bread. When 'Cooks' was sounded at 11.45 the
Caterer Boy in charge went to the mess and the Cook Boy
went to the galley and brought the food to the mess and
between them they cut it up and put it out so that there was
some on each plate. The Petty Officer Boy or Caterer Boy,
with the bully boy, sat next to the ship's side and the other
boys down each side of the table. When 'Dismiss' was
sounded all the boys went to their messes and stood up to
attention while the Instructors looked to see that the rations
were distributed equally and on many occasions the caterer
and bully boys were made to leave their dinner and come to
the end of the table. All the other boys moved up one place.
After that grace was said and 'Carry on' was ordered.

The foregoing is another instance of unchanging procedures
carried on through generations of boys under training: precisely
the same dinner-time rituals were followed, including the
unequal-portions remedy, as already mentioned, fifty years on.

Our only utensils were a tin plate, an earthenware basin, knife,
fork and tablespoon. If we lost any, money was stopped out of
our pay. After dinner our Instructor took us all over the ship
and explained a good many things and although it was very
cold made us go up the rigging and during the afternoon told
us we were to join our own part of the ship.
     6.30 a.m. next day it was my part of the ship to bath, so as
soon as you had stowed your hammock, you had to undress
and go naked on the upper deck and bath in cold water . . .
and looked over by an Instructor when you were finished to

see if you were clean; all this on a frosty morning protected by only a small canvas windscreen with only a small coarse towel to dry yourself on. After, breakfast – dry bread and a piece of fat pork, tea without milk and a very little sugar (if any). I have to say now that every Instructor carried his 'stonnachie', a cane or a piece of rope, and one man I remember very well always carried a genang stick around with him, a piece of ash about three feet six inches long and about three-quarters of an inch in diameter and when he hit you with it you knew all about it. All the while I was there the food was poor, punishment severe and stoppage of pay rife, we were paid sixpence a week on Thursday and when your number was called you had to take off you hat and hold it in front of you, top up, and say 'Thank you, sir!' always whether you got sixpence, threepence or 'Not Entitled' known as North Easter. Every boy had to learn to swim in a wooden bathing tray three feet six inches deep at the shallow end and about seven feet at the other and it was covered in barnacles. The method of teaching swimming was by two Instructors to each boy. The boy would have a three inch canvas strap round his waist with two lines attached. The Instructors would have a line each at the shallow end and persuade the boy to enter at the shallow end, keeping him afloat until he got out of his depth, and then one Instructor would let his line slacken or perhaps they both would slacken their lines, and the boy would be floundering about until they pulled him up again. I learned in about three lessons – with treatment like that you learn quickly.

Every Thursday afternoon, weather permitting, a bumboat man would come alongside selling pieces of bread pudding, a penny a time, and little bags of sweets. The boys were kept hungry and used to write home for stamps and these were legal tender with the bumboat man.

Every morning, except Saturday and Sunday, the decks were scrubbed and dried whatever the weather, except rain or snow, and it was darned cold when it was freezing. Saturday, the upper deck was always holystoned and kneeling on a sandy deck pushing holystones backwards and forwards was hardly a pleasure and meant a lot of sore knees. We were never allowed

to wear boots and socks unless we were dressed in No. 1 suits
or were going ashore.

   Punishment was severe, and caning was given for the most
trivial offences, most frequent was for smoking in the heads or
swearing. Most days there was punishment. I witnessed two
birchings while I was on HMS 'Ganges'. One was of six strokes
and one of twelve. We always knew when there was going to
be a birching because the birch, an instrument just like a
besom, was brought up from the stores a day beforehand and
placed over the coppers in the ship's galley to become pliable.
When there was a birching the Captain read out the Articles of
War pertaining to the offence and the boy was strapped over
the bits, his hands and feet tied so that he could not move. His
trousers were then pulled down and a man of about thirty-five,
about twelve stone, would apply the birch with all the strength
and venom he could muster. I can still see the boy after his
twelve strokes, his bottom like a piece of raw beef. At the end of
the twelve strokes the lad was released but he was in such
distress he had to be carried down to the sick bay for attention.
How long he stayed there I do not know but I can still picture
it to this day. The 'Ganges' cannot be compared to HMS
'Impregnable' at Devonport or HMS 'St Vincent' at Portsmouth
because whereas these two ships could always get their stores
and supplies, the 'Ganges' depended a lot on the weather for
food and water.

   The daily routine was almost the same. Up at 6 a.m. Scrub
deck till 8 a.m. Breakfast, Divisions and Prayers, then
instructions till dinner time with ten minutes break for stand
easy. After dinner, more instruction till 4 p.m. Then tea, five
o'clock evening quarters and inspection. Dismissed around 6
p.m. After that the evenings were your own.

An astonishing number of not just similar but identical terms,
routines and procedures are apparent in this account to anyone
familiar with the HMS *Ganges* of fifty, even sixty years later, long
after the rest of the world had moved on. Scrubbing out followed
by morning Divisions; dishing-up of dinner and the gabbled
grace; brutal swimming instructions; harsh punishments . . . it is
easier to list the few things which had changed – not all for the

better. Meals improved somewhat, or rather provisions did, but in the immediate post-Second World War Navy food was atrociously cooked and crudely served. The curious greasy, bitter cocoa was still being served up as an early-morning bowel starter fifty years on. Perhaps there existed a victualling-yard somewhere with a vast warehouse full of the stuff, spoils of some long-ago Gold Coast punitive expedition. A rattan cane replaced the birch, but ceremonial thrashings were as freely administered and resulted in the same bruised and lacerated buttocks; twelve strokes was still the maximum permitted.

The regime aboard *Ganges* hulk in 1898 would seem spartan enough, but as old sailors are wont to claim, 'It doesn't blow like it used to', and there was plenty of criticism of the 'pampering' of boys from old hands who had learned their trade the hard way – on the job, with a bosun's mate's ropes-end as tutor. The following is from an anonymous pamphlet dated 1877:[10]

A few years ago the system of training boys might be fitly and simply described as one of cruelty; the most trifling offence met with a severe rope-ending, while anything approaching a crime was certain to bring the offender to the breech of a gun and the cat. Boys just shipped were mustered (often in bitter cold weather) almost naked on the upper deck, their hands blistered with a cane, and they were then ordered over the mast-head; petty officers concerned with their training were armed with a stout cane, and reprimanded if they did not use it freely; but a change became necessary, for the matter had not merely reached the public ear, but had actually become notorious, and parents hesitated to send their children to sea in Her Majesty's Navy. A change was accordingly made, not a modification of the old system, but a revolution from cruelty to pampering. A boy in the present day has no conception of discipline until he is rated ordinary seaman; the utmost latitude is permitted him, punishment is the exception, in order that the books may bear a favourable comparison with those of other training-ships, and so far from the petty officers being ordered to carry and use canes, they are now not allowed (on pain of great displeasure) to even speak harshly; but should a petty officer so far forget himself as to wound the feelings of a boy in the latter particular, he is certain to be punished for it; and in our training-ships instances are of daily occurrence in which a petty officer is publicly reprimanded in the presence of all the boys for some real or imaginary offence. Under this system (or, no system) the instructor loses all control over those beneath him; the boy reaches the age of eighteen, is rated a man, has forgotten even the mild discipline of going to bed supperless, and sees no reason why additional restraints should be placed upon him, now that he is, in Service parlance, and in his own opinion, a man. . . .

This diatribe may be taken with a pinch of the same old salt who wrote it: such attitudes to nurture and discipline smack more of the 1960s than the 1870s, and would seem to have regressed entirely to the bad old days in the few years to Boy Austin's tribulations. It is, of course, a flight of fancy, as is the following in similar vein, also anonymous:

In the training-ship did not the instructor have to wash his clothes, and even hang them on the line for him? So that now his troubles really begin, they seem to be severe, and discontent follows. Why should he render obedience to a man of the same rank as his late instructor – a man who wears the same device on his arm in worsted as he himself wore when a boy in gold, and further, a man who at the present moment may be his messmate? Discontent is succeeded by impertinence and impertinence to (sic) insubordination; that which in the training ship would have passed by as not worth heeding is now considered and treated as a crime. From small offences to large ones the road is very short and easy, and thus we soon find him striking the petty officer for whom he has learned so little respect; prison follows, and now his character having been blackened for the remainder of his Service career, what can we expect but that he will continue in the same course until brought to a court-martial and turned out of the Service, having succeeded in costing the country £95, and disseminating his bad example among those of his companions who may as yet be not altogether irreclaimable.

Given the abundance of contemporaneous testimony to the respect, and often fear, felt by training-ship boys towards their instructors, this florid and highly imaginative portrait of a nautical *Rake's Progress* could only have been regarded with derision at the time.

In 1904 the *Ganges* hulk was towed from Falmouth to Harwich in anticipation of the construction of a shore barracks at Shotley, which was officially opened on 4 October 1905. Shotley Barracks was the first and largest of the shore establishments built expressly for the training of boys, eventually replacing the hulks which were becoming increasingly insanitary, and which could not supply the training required by a modern navy. Initially, new-entrant boys spent three months in the barracks before being transferred to *Ganges* hulk now at moorings in Shotley creek and renamed *Ganges II*. One of them recalled:

The 'Ganges' was a lovely place; it was like a public school. You had dormitories, beds; you had a laundry. You see you got the taste of that and then you went to a ship! The only boys that stopped there were the Signal Boys and the Sparker Boys. The Seaman Boys did three months at Shotley Barracks and then went to the 'Ganges II', the old 'hulk' and you had a bit of a time there! They used to chase you over the mast. We had Marine Instructors – Blue Marines[11] – and they were cruel swine. They used to carry a bit of rubber and the last one over always got a bit of stonnachie – I was never last! The same on the messdeck. They used to chase you off the messdeck and the Crushers used to stand at the bottom with the cane and the last one always got it. You didn't get his in Shotley Barracks itself.[12]

By this date, 'over the mast' was merely an exercise in agility, courage and a head for heights on a ship's mast bare of sails. Sail drill had been discontinued by an *Admiralty Circular* of March 1903 which enjoined that 'Physical and mechanical training is to be largely substituted for mast and sail drill and such other drills as are not suited for the modern Seamen'. So perhaps life was, after all, a little less hard for the new boy; doubtless Holman and Humphreys would have thought so. There were opponents of

the change in high places, too (no quip intended). Lord Brassey –
not a naval officer but a keen amateur sailor, a civil lord of the
Admiralty and founder of the *Naval Annual* – wrote in that
publication, in 1905: '. . . it seems regrettable that all masted
ships should have disappeared from the training service for
boys. Stationary ships are now mastless; the brigs are paid
off . . . physical drill in the gymnasium is not a satisfactory
substitute for training aloft'. Similar protests from senior
officers, serving and retired, and influential civilians like Lord
Brassey were not prompted wholly by nostalgia: the Royal Navy
was alone among major sea-powers in abolishing sail-training
for its cadets and young seamen; it continues in some fleets to
the present day. But Admiral of the Fleet Lord 'Jackie' Fisher
was bent on dragging the Navy into the twentieth century and
this was one among his many reforms. On the issue of training
aloft however, in a rare compromise, he ordered the erection of
a 140-foot mast on the Shotley parade ground. A century or so
later, and twenty-five years since the barracks was abandoned
by the Navy, the famous *Ganges* mast remains a prominent
Suffolk landmark, towering over a police training college. The
mast itself has been classified a listed building, regularly
maintained and refitted at public expense.

After the privations of a training hulk, Shotley Barracks may
well have seemed, by comparison, a 'lovely place'. But still some
were driven by the harsh regime to attempt escape, despite the
practical certainty of recapture followed by the mandatory
flogging:

> One night my chum said to me, 'I can't stick this'. We made it
> look as if we were sleeping in our beds, we had to turn in at
> eight or nine at night, and we hopped over the fence and away
> down towards Ipswich – not on the road but down by the river
> Orwell. The only way to Ipswich is between the river Orwell
> and the river Stour. First we saw the Marine walking up and
> down guarding the barracks and so, as he turned round, we
> lay down in the grass, and as he turned the other way we got a
> bit further. When we thought we were well out of sight of him
> we came to a big stream about ten feet across; we made a jump
> for it and landed right in the middle and got soaking wet

through. After that we careered up the road for about ten miles until four o'clock in the morning. They had informed the Police and everything and we saw nobody, until with only two or three miles to go we spotted a bloke on a bicycle. We didn't know he was a policeman until he got pretty near so we hopped over the hedge and across a field but he caught us and took us back. We were made to go and bath in cold water out in the courtyard. This was in February. They put us in cells with one blanket and told us to sleep; that was *four* o'clock in the morning! We were taken before the Commander and he ordered six cuts with the cane. We were put across the horse with just a pair of white trousers and nothing else, and he wealed us from one side to the other and cut the skin.[13]

Fifty years on, desperate boys still sometimes 'ran'; rarely got as far as Ipswich before recapture (the location of Shotley Barracks had been chosen with care); were returned to be placed in cells and to receive six cuts in the morning; twelve for a second offence. Six or twelve, the resulting lacerations usually required treatment in the sick bay. Even the Royal Navy made some concessions to social enlightenment, however – by 1947 floggings were no longer administered in public. They were carried out in a small room (but big enough to swing a cat in) attached to the cell block in the presence of the Commander, an MO and a Royal Marine police corporal, with the Master-at-Arms plying the cane. Shotley boys believed that the 'Jaunty' received an honorarium of half-a-crown for each flogging he administered. They had no proof of this, but felt that it would explain the enthusiasm and vigour with which he laid it on.

To return to 1906:

The Instructors in the 'Ganges' were not too bad but there were two – Sinclair, who was never happy unless he was banging some boy, and the Gunnery Instructor, Smith. He had some private trouble of his own but he was not as bad as Sinclair. I used to say that even if I met Sinclair on crutches, I'd kick away the crutches and bang him. I never saw him again, which was, perhaps, as well. There was no check on the Instructors, and looking back on it, that was the error of it.

There was no justice at all, because if you complained to the Officer of the Division you were quite likely to get put in the Commander's Report on a charge, which could be trumped up against you and that might mean six cuts with the cane.

Thus speaks Boy Henry Minchin and many shared his experience of ill-treatment without redress. Then as later, the striking of boys by their instructors was officially forbidden but unofficially condoned. Minchin never forgot:

There was no justice then, and I often said that if I ever got in a position to check it, I would do so. As it happened I did. I became Master-at-Arms at the 'St Vincent' Boys' Training establishment and I was able to suppress it. A man can do his duty and chase the youngsters around and make them do what they were told when they were told. That was one side of the question which was proved out and out and came in very useful during action. The old saying used to be, 'If you are the last man left alive, you go on firing, as the last show may decide the battle.' But there was no need for the brutality.[14]

The Master-at-Arms was the senior rating of a ship or shore establishment, the Navy's equivalent of the Regimental Sergeant-Major, and it was upon this petty officer's quality and character that the happiness and efficiency of a ship's company largely depended. Lucky the ship with a 'Jaunty' who was fair and impartial, and who knew and cared about what went on. Not all were so fortunate.

The traditional Navy attitude to discipline is summed up by that rare specimen – later to become even rarer – the ex-lower decker risen to wardroom rank, commissioned during the First World War:

I used to dislike a lot of petty things. If you incurred the displeasure of one of the Petty Officers he would have it in for you but I managed to keep my nose clean. If you kick your foot against a wall, you're going to hurt your foot. If you put yourself against discipline you're going to get hurt – nobody else. On a well-disciplined ship you knew what you had to do.

Unfortunately some ships were a bit lax but with a disciplined ship if you went against things you knew something would happen. My opinion and my experience was that the disciplined ships I was in were always the happy ones, because you knew what you were doing. I think the majority of POs and Chiefs of my time would confirm this.[15]

This view was unexceptional and commonly held among naval officers, though it should be said that some of the happiest and most efficient ships' companies were those serving in small ships such as destroyers and submarines, in which discipline was more relaxed and informal, though no less real and effective in action.

All things come to an end, even boys' training. Earlier, trained boys were drafted direct to a ship of the Fleet, or to a receiving ship to await such draft. By the turn of the century however a training squadron had been formed, consisting of half-a dozen armoured cruisers – 'ironclads' – whose function was to provide boys with practical sea-going experience; putting into practice the seamanship and gunnery drills they had learned in the hulks. Each class of trainees was taken on a cruise of, if they were lucky, the Mediterranean; more often, a circumnavigation of the British Isles. After a year in a hulk or shore barracks most boys were keen to get to sea, which after all was what they had joined for, and most enjoyed the experience once they had got their sea legs. In this they were given every assistance.

I really enjoyed the training trips. After you had learnt the theory in Shotley and then to come aboard and use it to fire the guns and rifles, heaving the lead, and the helm and all that sort of thing – it was really good. I never regretted that I had taken the step of joining the Navy except when I left England for the first time.[16]

That qualification refers to a rough crossing of the Bay of Biscay during which the captain stopped the ship for twenty-four-hours, allowing it to roll, bucket and wallow in a heavy swell until most of the trainees were prostrate with seasickness.

It was all an exciting novelty, those first few weeks at sea. In the training squadron the boys were supervised by a full staff of instructors; their daily routine, feeding and accommodation continued to be ordered for them, as it had been in barracks. It was only when, training finally over, they joined a Fleet ship as members of the ship's company that their troubles began.

> There were only eight of us boys. We had a little mess forward and we used to look after ourselves – nobody used to nurse us. We were issued with food – beef and so on – but we often didn't draw it or put it up properly and so we had a piece of bread instead. Next day when you got up at six in the morning and came down to the mess you were lucky if you got a mug of tea. We didn't have cups and saucers then, just basins and not too many of them because we used to break them and many a time I have drunk out of the tea urn. Very often we didn't get anything till dinner, and, of course, tea was only bread and marge and supper was bread and marge. I suppose I was a boy in that ship for nearly a year and I always remember the first dinner I had in a broadside mess[17] – a pot-mess of pork![18]

If true, this is a sorry tale indeed and a grave reflection on the ship's officers and petty officers. Victuals in warships were traditionally issued raw to each individual mess, rationed according to the number in the mess. They then had to be prepared for cooking by the mess's duty 'cook' who was not, of course, a cook, and put up to the ship's galley for cooking. Then and later, boys (or adult entrants for that matter) were given no instruction on food preparation during their training; the *Admiralty Manual of Seamanship*, Volume I, issued to all boys, did not include a section on cookery. It was learned by trial and error and by suffering the wrath of messmates when the food was ruined. In practice, a 'green' hand joining a mess would have his first culinary efforts guided and supervised by older men. But boys were messed separately, and it would appear that the boy quoted above was drafted to a small warship – probably a sloop or gunboat – as there were only eight boys carried. Bigger ships, which might have had forty or fifty boys in their complements, would detail a leading seaman or old AB to act as mess caterer. Those boys should not have been left to fend for themselves.

A lower-deck critic of the messing system in the early 1900s wrote:

The standard rations were served out; meat hacked from the carcass by an amateur butcher, potatoes, bread, tea, sugar and milk (tinned). At certain times flour and raisins were issued, and when the meat was what is still termed 'potmess meat', onions too were supplied. The rest had to be bought. There is no doubt the sailor had to be a handyman, for just as the Israelites had to make bricks without straw, so the pre-war naval man had to make his meals from joints of meat and anything else he could get hold of. Where a messmate was found who could serve up a good dinner, he was considered a find.

The duties of the 'cook of the mess' started generally after tea, when the first preparations for the next day's dinner were made; straight bake, sea-pie, oosh, oosh with an awning over, in other words, a pie. With this particular dish mistakes were made many times, especially if the cook-of-the-mess forgot to tally it, for after spending a long time trying to make a light flaky pastry, it eventually got steamed, which meant it was cooked in the copper over the vegetables, so that with pastry meant for baking but steamed, and tasting of vegetables, the mess had rather a questionable dinner.

This incident is a prime illustration of the brainlessness, or perhaps cussedness, of the naval 'Slushy'. The author recalls a similar one where the duty cook of the mess, in the mistaken belief that it was one of the rare days when the galley was deep-frying, chipped the potatoes for dinner. They came back boiled to a pulp in the mess's 'spud net'.

Generally once a week it was Potmess, a name which requires a good deal of understanding, for in the event of the mess getting that part of a bullock just behind the hindquarters, that is, the neck of the next one, it required a mess in a pot to satisfy the appetite of one's messmates. Luckily for the cook, perhaps, in a great many cases, his messmates did not really know what was in it. A favourite move was to have an accident with the curry powder as this covered a multitude of sins.[19]

This system of victualling was virtually unchanged since Nelson's day, and it continued so until the 1920s and well into the post-war years in small ships. Here it was known as 'canteen messing'; such provisions as meat, flour, potatoes, tea, sugar and tinned milk were issued from ship's stores; in addition a small per capita allowance was made for the purchase of such 'luxuries' as eggs, fruit, tinned vegetables and so on from the ship's canteen. At the end of a quarter, any balance of this victualling allowance unspent was paid out to the mess caterer or leading hand. The system gave rise to much abuse: healthy, growing boys and young seamen had commensurate appetites, while the mess was ruled by old hands more interested in beer-money than food, accustomed to breafasting on 'a cup of tea and a Woodbine' and in harbour, usually absent on shore leave at supper-time. In such a mess midday dinner was the only sustaining meal of the day, and the youngster was driven to spending his own money at the canteen to feed himself.

Many boys, unlucky in their draft, were disappointed to find themselves rather worse off in the Fleet than in their training-ships, not only in the matter of food; also through lack of supervision and consequent bullying by adult ratings. A Boy Seaman aboard ship called everybody 'sir', from captain to AB. His officers generally ignored him, except when he transgressed.

Our Captain was a Captain Blunt. He was a little man, wore a beard, a proper Captain Kettle. He was a pretty cute customer for discipline. I got six cuts of the cane from him, for something that I really shouldn't have got it for. At that time, spitting on the deck was a heinous crime and I was the First Lieutenant's messenger and we were getting out the steam boat and I was standing there without anything to do and this First Lieutenant told me to 'Give a hand boy! Give a hand!' for she had a bit of a list and it was quite a job to push her out. Well, being a youngster, I got right opposite where the boiler was. The funnel was down but the fire was lit and I got a mouthful of this and I spat it out and Jimmy put me in the rattle and I got put in Captain's Report and then six cuts of the cane for that. They had a torpedo tube on the upper deck almost abaft and that's where I had it. You had a pair of duck trousers on, nothing underneath and lying over this hammock. The Jaunty, he was a pretty hefty bloke, and they had a heavy cane and I had six lovely wows on my backside and that was a green rub, really, but in those days you couldn't say anything about that. But I bit my cap. I never yelled. One of the Signal Boys got six at the same time, but he got six for thieving out of an Officer's cabin and he deserved it not me. I think everybody in the ship's company was in sympathy with me but they couldn't do nothing.[20]

Mollycoddling of juveniles was never one of the Royal Navy's failings. The same harshness was evinced towards adolescent officers, the cadets and midshipmen (though perhaps not quite equally) whose bullying by their seniors in the gunroom has been widely recorded. Junior midshipmen could also be caned, and were, by the sub-lieutenant, the gunroom's head prefect. Little wonder then, that having jumped through those particular hoops themselves, few naval officers concerned themselves overmuch with the tribulations of boy ratings. Parallels between the treatment of boy-sailors and boy-officers should not be overdrawn, however. The young gentlemen had marine servants to look after them and their kit, and their food left little to be desired; a Dartmouth cadet of the time breakfasted on porridge, omelette or buttered eggs, ham and tongue.[21] This repast bears comparison with the slice-and-scrape breakfast of the training-ship boys, but not much.

We cannot leave a chapter on the Dreadnoughts without mention of the thing that loomed so large in the lives of all steam-age sailors: the thoroughly-hated evolution of 'coal ship'. Coal was the lifeblood of the ship, which without it was so many thousand tons of useless metal. Whenever a warship put to sea, if only for a few hours, her first priority on return to base was to refill her bunkers; this took precedence over all else. The entire ship's company, except essential watchkeepers such as duty signalmen and boats' crews and including junior officers, on the pipe 'Coal Ship!' turned-to, dressed in their oldest clothing, as the colliers came alongside. Coal was shovelled into bags, swung inboard, trundled along the waist on barrows and shot into the bunker-hatches, where the stokers toiled frantically in the blind, choking darkness to trim it. On deck, a black cloud of coal-dust gradually thickened and settled on everything and everybody. The ship's boys, deemed to lack a man's strength, were sent down into the collier's holds for the comparatively light labour of holding open the sacks for filling. Few escaped cutting and bruising to their hands, protective gloves not being an item on any supply officer's stores list.

> The worst part of coaling ship was after coaling because then the ship had to be washed down from truck to keel, before you could go and try to wash yourself. Everything – masts, funnels – had to be washed down with the hoses. There was nowhere the dust didn't get. In the 'Mars' you had to rig the coal chutes[22] and the Seamen even had to trim the bunkers.

The aftermath of coaling was universally the most hated part of the whole filthy business, and the boys suffered with the rest:

> In the 'Queen Mary' we used to take twenty-three hundred tons aboard and that was horrible. Us Signal Boys used to supply the bags and it did depend on what duty you were on. After Coal Ship you had to clean up and you then had to go and have a bath and there was absolutely no room as everyone wanted one at the same time. There wasn't enough water to go round and you got on as well as you could. Your coaling rig you used to bundle up and stow away somewhere and then wash it whenever you could. If you were lucky enough you could wash it after coaling but then where were you going to hang it? Even on those days some of the Instructors wanted to muster you and see if you had washed the coal out of your ears![23]

Most boys would have preferred working aloft on sails and rigging to coaling ship (or would have said so if asked at the time!) but this particular bane of a Boy Seaman's existence was to be comparatively short-lived, with conversion to oil-fuel beginning in the second decade of the century. The ultra-traditionalist Royal Navy was no enemy of scientific progress where the matter of fighting efficiency was concerned; only in its treatment of ratings in general and its boys in particular. No progress there. . . .

FOUR

Shotley

The HMS *Ganges* which I joined in the bitterly cold January of 1947 was a land-girt 'stone frigate' rather than a sailing ship hulk, but how much else had changed in half a century, the reader may judge. I may say that an ex-*Ganges* boy, on joining the Fleet, was regarded by ratings who had joined the Navy as adults with a mixture of pity and awe. There were other boys' training establishments, but *Ganges* was the byword.

Let me begin with a narrative, after the manner of Humphreys, Riley, Noble and the rest, of my reception and initiation into the Royal Navy in that dawn of the atomic age. . . .

It was late evening when the train pulled in to Ipswich station, a piercingly cold night with a powdering of frozen snow in the wind-gusts, harbinger of the arctic winter ahead. Cold, cramped and hungry, we tumbled out on to the deserted, dimly lit platform; forty or so of us. Carriage doors slammed, a whistle chirrupped and, creaking and hissing, the train slid off into the darkness. As its tail lamp disappeared, a voice hailed us:

'*Ganges* draft! Come on then, let's be having you!'

A figure stood in the pool of light at the ticket barrier, beckoning. We shuffled towards it, carrying our motley luggage.

'Right, form two ranks along here – chop, chop, the sooner we get you sorted the sooner you'll be out of the cold!'

I could see now that this self-possessed individual with the air of authority was a slightly built youth scarcely older than ourselves, whose uniform was hidden under a glistening black oilskin, beneath which were visible snow-white blancoed gaiters and boots whose glassy surfaces reflected the lamps in the station yard. When we had formed two ragged lines under the canopy, he called the roll from a clipboard held up to the feeble lighting.

A couple of names were not answered to, their owners presumably having had second thoughts and doing a side-shuffle at Liverpool Street.

In the coming weeks, I was to wish fervently that I had had the wit to do likewise. . . .

We clambered into the two Royal Navy four-tonners awaiting us in the station forecourt and drove through empty town streets giving way to utterly dark country roads, jolting and swaying and bracing our tired limbs to keep our seats on the slatted wooden benches. At last we slowed and swung between an imposing pair of wrought-iron gates embellished with much gilding and the Admiralty's foul-anchor badge bearing the date '1905'. As we ground slowly along a tarmac road I craned forward to glimpse through the open tailgate a huge ship's figurehead in the form of a turbanned and bejewelled blackamoor, scowling fiercely, its gaudy colours accentuated by floodlighting.

At length the lorry pulled up and we were ordered to disembark. We found ourselves standing in a sort of gravelled quadrangle with verandahed corrugated-iron huts ranged on three sides, the fourth occupied by a brick building and a tall flagstaff. Our youthful supervisor led us into one of the huts. The interior was brightly lit, warm and furnished with long wooden tables and benches. It was filled with cooking smells and we needed no second bidding to take a place at the tables. Each place was set with knife and fork, a metal plate and a battered metal cup, the last two – rather superfluously, I remember thinking – embossed with a broad arrow and the initials 'G.R.', which particular 'G' not vouchsafed. White-aproned and hatted cooks appeared, bearing large metal trays of sausages and chips and 'fannies' of thick, greasy, unsweetened cocoa. There followed much metallic clattering as plates and mugs were passed up and back again, laden. I remember how much I enjoyed that first Navy meal, despite the penitentiary quality of the tableware. A middle-aged (in naval terms, late thirties) petty officer now appeared and took charge of us. We were hustled to a barrack-room barely furnished with two rows of iron-framed beds, each with a thin, canvas-covered mattress, a pillow and three folded

blankets. We were ordered to dump our things on a bed and 'get
fell in outside, chop chop!' This was widely-used Navalese for
'Hurry!', imported perhaps from the China Station. Then we
performed a ragged, out-of-step march across the quadrangle to
another hut marked 'Clothing Store'. Inside, a wooden counter
ran the length of the room on which, his uniform cap all but
brushing the ceiling, stood a very tall naval officer. At intervals
behind the counter stood half a dozen or so Wrens in white
blouses and navy-blue slacks, looking rather tired and
disgruntled under the bright strip-lighting; unsurprising
considering the lateness of the hour – now nearly midnight. The
officer introduced himself as Mr Barnes, Gunner Royal Navy.
Unlike the Wrens, he was remarkably breezy and cheerful.

'Come along you lucky lads', he cajoled us, 'don't hang back,
it's all free! Right. When I sing out an item of kit make sure you
get it. One kitbag. . . .'

A large tube of heavy white canvas was dumped on the
counter in front of each of us. Multifarious items followed in
quick succession, in response to the gunner's litany: socks,
sailors' vests cut square at the neck and apparently called
'flannels'; underpants of a beigeish colour and curious cut, knee-
length and buttoned at the waist. The Cockney wags directed
hopefully funny remarks at the Wrens, receiving withering looks
in return.

'Handkerchiefs, blue bundle, two.'

'Square, black silk, two.'

'Collars, blue-jean, two.'

'Hatbox, black japanned, one.'

With our kitbags bulging, we came to:

'Jumper, blue serge, number three, men dressed as seamen,
one.'

'Trousers, ditto, pairs, one.'

At which, the Wrens, as one girl, reached up to draw a canvas
curtain across their side of the counter. The gunner instructed us
to try on these last two. 'The jumper goes over your head, if you
can get into it, it fits. Sing out if you can't'. I got into mine
without difficulty, there was slack to spare, and hauled on the
trousers which buttoned across the stomach and had no flies but
a large flap which let down in front. There appeared to be no

pockets in either garment. I eyed my companions and saw no resemblance at all to the saucy, dashing Jack Tars on shore leave in town streets. The lad next to me in the line-up presented a particularly risible appearance; he was tall, taller even than Mr Barnes, and gangling. The sleeves of his jumper ended inches above his bony wrists and his 'bell-bottoms' flapped at half-mast round his lean shins. This was the best they could do for him; the Navy had not allowed for six feet two of Boy Seaman. Poor 'Bugs' Bailey, doomed to mockery for all his time at Shotley, until made-to-measure 'sea suits' were issued before our graduation to the Fleet a year hence. As if that were not enough, 'Bugs' had lost his front teeth in some encounter or other and whenever he grinned, which was surprisingly often in the circumstances, his ill-fitting denture dropped on to his lower lip, giving him the appearance of a mentally retarded hare. He was the butt of all, messmates and instructors alike, for the next twelve months, but he had whatever it takes to cope with it, unlike some others, and was widely popular.

At last we trooped out, back across the parade ground to the dormitory; caps perched anyhow on our heads, stiff new boots slung by their laces about our necks, grappling our bulging kitbags to keep them out of the snow which had now settled to a depth of 3 or 4 inches and still fell steadily. The petty officer waited there to receive us together with the boy-in-authority whom the PO addressed as 'Instructor Boy'. The latter had doffed his oilskin, and I saw that he wore on his left sleeve a red worsted chevron surmounted by a small crown and foul-anchor. There were other grades of Petty Officer Boys which will be referred to later.

We were instructed to dump our kit by our beds and turn in, which we were glad to do. It had been a long day.

After a sound sleep, despite the cold hut, we were roused at 7 a.m., an hour later than Shotley's normal reveille as a concession to our delayed retirement, and given a mug of the same greasy, sugarless cocoa which accompanied our supper the night before, and two hard-tack biscuits. Our induction then began. Most of the ensuing few days need not be recounted here in much detail as the procedures are familiar and common to all services; the inoculations, the close-to-the-bone haircuts, the chaplain's little chat, the introduction to parade-ground drill. The snow stopped falling, and froze. Time was found in our full days to form working-parties to shovel the snow from our immediate environs.

These now became clearer to us. We were housed in an annexe to the main establishment, known as Cornwell Division, after Boy Jackie Cornwell VC, the famous boy-hero of Jutland and our exemplar. The annexe was located down a short road some quarter-mile from *Ganges* proper, to which we were marched on numerous occasions for visits to the sick bay, barber-shop and so on, which gave us ample opportunity to survey our home for the next year. HMS *Ganges* was dominated by its great mast, firmly cemented in the parade-ground and rising to a height of 143 feet precisely. It was fully rigged with yards, shrouds and ratlines and was to loom large in our Shotley lives. It was not, as we supposed, the mainmast of the original HMS *Ganges*, a wooden wall launched at Bombay in 1821, but a bastardized erection made up of the lower foremast of one Victorian ironclad and the upper mizzen of another (the figurehead referred to earlier was, however, that of the old *Ganges*). A large White Ensign was hoisted on the gaff during daylight hours and gaudy bunting fluttered from the yardarms most days, including Nelson's immortal 'England expects . . .' on every 21 October.

At the opposite end of the vast parade-ground stood a long, low, modern red-brick block of 1930s vintage which was the chiefs and petty officers' mess; with this one exception, the establishment dated to the turn of the century. Occupying the length of the west side was the drill shed, an enormous, hangar-like building lit by large windows along its length, empty save for a collection of ships' figureheads and crests around the walls, faded group photographs of Victorian naval officers draped over and around muzzle-loading great guns, and an enormous wooden board displaying, in elaborate red lettering, every last stanza of Kipling's 'If'. The drill shed was used to accommodate parades in wet weather.

Two covered walkways extended from the parade-ground east to the foreshore opposite Harwich harbour; one was longer than the other and they were known respectively as the 'long covered way' and the 'short covered way'. Off these, at intervals along their lengths, like the teeth of a comb, were the boys' messes, described in detail later. Other buildings of note were the seamanship block, the gunnery school (with both of which we were to become all too familiar), the gymnasium and swimming bath, the signals school standing high on Shotley Point and reached by the three long flights of stone stairs of evil reputation known as Faith, Hope and Charity; and lastly, the sick quarters, really a small but fully equipped cottage hospital in its own grounds, in which stood a wooden bungalow to lodge the next-of-kin of dangerously ill boys. Somewhere in the immediate countryside could be seen the captain's considerable house and demesne, though we boys never saw this Mount Olympus, and could not have said precisely where it was. At the bottom of the long covered way, extending out into the Haven, was Shotley Pier with its picket-boats and long trots of cutters and whalers.

ORGANIZATION

Routine in the boys' training establishments was organized in five-week cycles. Every fifth week throughout the year, save for leave periods, a fresh draft of recruits[1] arrived. These were housed in the annexe under strict quarantine; contact with other boys and ship's company apart from our own instructors was strictly forbidden and entry into the main establishment was only in organized parties. Each of the three terms lasted fifteen weeks; on course, examinations were held at ten, twenty and thirty weeks. Boys on course were organized into divisions, messes and classes. There were six divisions (apart from Cornwell, the new entrants), named after famous admirals: Anson, Blake, Collingwood, Drake, Grenville and Hawke – Nelson was conspicuously absent, though his famous spirit was much commended to us and another of his signals was emblazoned in foot-high brass letters over the portals of the Gunnery School: ENGAGE THE ENEMY MORE CLOSELY. Shotley knew not radar.

There were three messes in each division with roughly forty boys to a mess, divided for instruction purposes into two classes according to academic ability previously determined at a simple three-Rs test in the annexe. The relatively brighter were placed in the advanced class and sported a small worsted star on the left sleeve (one AC boy on home leave, asked by his girlfriend what it signified, claimed to be an astronomer's mate). The relative dullards formed the general class. It should be emphasized that none of us was all that academically bright or, presumably, we would have been elsewhere. Both classes followed the same training curriculum, except that the AC boys spent rather longer on schoolwork, being coached for an educational certificate, possession of which led to early rating to Ordinary Seaman, an objective much to be desired. The structure was such that each division included a mess, with its two classes, at each 10-week point of the curriculum; ten, twenty and thirty weeks, with finals and passing-out at forty weeks. I refer here to the Boy Seaman training course; the Signal Boys and Boy Telegraphists spent several months longer at Shotley before joining the Fleet. The top 20 per cent of mark-scorers in the educational test were offered the Signals Branch but some, for the foregoing reason, opted to be seamen. There was a generous annual leave allowance of seven weeks; two each at Christmas and Easter with three weeks in the summer.

Divisions were headed by a divisional officer, usually a lieutenant but occasionally a lieutenant-commander, usually young and specially appointed to boys' training, an appointment which would be described in modern parlance as a good career move. The divisional officer inspected kits and accommodation at prescribed intervals, led his division on parade and encouraged divisional spirit in sporting activities. But the real power lay with the instructors, who were responsible for training and discipline – training not merely in seamanship and gunnery but in the Navy's way of doing things. There were two instructors to each mess, a chief petty officer and a petty officer, as a rule instructing in gunnery and seamanship respectively. The CPO was normally a chief gunner's mate; the PO might be of any specialism. It is necessary to explain that a Royal Navy seaman had two ratings, substantive and non-substantive, or 'left-arm' and 'right-arm', according to where the appropriate badges were worn. Thus a leading seaman (single foul-anchor on left sleeve), petty officer (crossed anchors and crown, likewise) and chief petty officer (three brass buttons horizontally across each cuff) held that rating and were clothed, accommodated, paid and endowed with disciplinary powers accordingly. In addition, a senior rating such as these could achieve advancement in his 'non-substantive' rating as a gunner, torpedoman, anti-submarine operator and many other categories open to seamen. His specialist badge was worn on the right arm, accruing the appropriate number of stars plus a crown as he advanced through the classes of his specialization, except in the case of a chief petty officer, who wore his branch badges on his lapels. So one or two messes might have had a PO gunner's mate (the highest gunnery rate) and a CPO with a low non-substantive rate who specialized in seamanship.

Both instructors were responsible for the cleanliness, good order and discipline of the boys in their charge, in and out of instructional hours. Out of hours, they took charge for twenty-four hours alternately, changing over at midday, dinner-time on the messdeck; likewise at weekends, every other on-duty. They were assisted by leading and petty officer boys, selected by the instructors themselves from among the trainees, who had been unobtrusively assessed for leadership qualities during their time in the annexe. Some instructors gave these boys considerable powers; if abused, as they sometimes were, they could be as summarily disrated, to face a terrible revenge. There was considerable rivalry between messes and divisions, engendered very largely by ambitious divisional officers, for sports trophies, spit-and-polish, examination marks (high), number of defaulters on commander's report (low) and in other areas. But the tone of any mess was set by the quality of its instructors.

INITIATION

The five-week isolation period in the annexe was utilized as a comparatively gentle introduction to life in *Ganges* proper. We were issued on joining with a printed list of 'Rules for the Guidance of Boys'. I still have mine. Rule 6 reads: 'Boys are on no account to enter any of the Ship's Company's Messes' (the 'Ship's Company' in *Ganges* were adult ratings of junior rank necessary to the day-to-day running of the establishment – cooks, stewards, stokers and so on). The inflexible naval rule that boys were never to mix with men, ashore or afloat, was no doubt a reflection of the second of Winston Churchill's three traditions of the Navy. Rule 7: 'Should a Boy receive any Money, Stamps or a Money Order from his friends or wish to save his Pocket Money, he is at once to take it to the Regulating Office. He is never to retain more than Two Shillings and Sixpence in his possession'. I have the card before me as I write and I notice that it is headed 'Revised June 1934'. The 'Two Shillings and Sixpence' (12½p) maximum still applied in 1947, so no account had been taken of inflation. And as that modest sum was in fact our total weekly pay, there was rarely a queue of pocket money-savers outside the Regulating Office. Rule 15 reads: 'Fighting, Quarrelling, Gambling, Tattooing, and the use of Bad Language are strictly forbidden; and as nearly all the punishments in a Man-of-War arise from Drinking, Boys are strongly advised to avoid the use of Intoxicating Liquors.'

This is the language of 1847 and made odd reading to me a century later. Speaking for myself, I had not the least inclination, leave aside the opportunity, to gamble, or get tattooed. During my time at Shotley quarrelling took place certainly, and it sometimes led to fighting, though no more I am sure than among any comparable group of young males at that date. The only concession to modernity (though this particular wheel has since spun full circle) was that references to contraband smoking materials had been inked out; smoking, subject to strictly enforced restrictions as to when and where, was now permitted if not encouraged.

There was much for us to learn in those first weeks: not least for those of us, the large majority, who were not ex-training ship boys or sea cadets, the mysteries of Jack Tar's archaic and complicated habiliments. On our first morning, immediately after the ritual shearing at the barber-shop, we were assembled in the mess-hall. Mr Barnes the Gunner was in charge and a mannequin had been detailed. This blushing lad stood on a table, clad in blue woollen jersey and bell-bottom trousers. First came the blue-jean collar, draped across the shoulders and secured below the ribcage by tapes. Then the serge jumper went over the head, was tugged into place and the collar hauled out from beneath it, so that its visible parts, edged with three narrow white strips, framed the chest and neck and hung down behind.

The next item was a black silk scarf, square in shape but folded to form a halter of the regulation width of two inches. This was tied behind the neck, under the collar. Its bight was secured by braid tapes already attached to the jumper at the base of its V-neck, the ends of which were cut to form swallowtails. The tapes were to be tied with a reef bow, and below the bow was to be left two fingers'-width of black silk. The last thing to go over the head was the lanyard. This was simply a white cord made into a loop with a slip-knot. It went under the collar and silk, the knot being positioned precisely over the breastbone, with the loose end looped behind the tapes and tucked inside the jumper. Its purpose was not explained to us, and no-one ventured to enquire. The old-time tar must have carried something on the end of it; a whistle or knife, perhaps. Whatever its original function, it was now just something else to keep clean and to vex us when struggling and fumbling to be properly dressed by the time 'Hands fall-in' was piped.

Finally, the cap. The sailor's round cap is a familiar enough article of headgear not to require a detailed description. We had been issued with no fewer than three: two with blue tops and one white. At that date the Admiralty decreed that summer began on the first day of May, and on that day, as any inhabitant of a dockyard town will testify, Navy personnel – officers, petty officers and ratings – all sported white tops to their caps. On the first of October, summer being deemed to have ended, caps reverted to navy-blue, inciting cries from irreverent urchins of 'Taxi!' Needless to say, there was a right and several wrong ways of wearing the cap. 'You don't have it flat-a-back Jack me hearty fashion', admonished the gunner, 'nor perched on the eyebrows like a pimple on a pig's arse.' It was to be worn straight and level on the head, the 'cap-tally' or ribbon bearing the ship's name to be tied with a neat bow above the left ear (tying a cap-tally neatly was something of an art, and the instructor boy showed us how, just once).

This, our uniform, was colloquially known as 'square rig', worn by junior ratings of the seaman, stoker and signals branches. Chiefs and petty officers and miscellaneous ratings such as cooks, stewards, supply assistants and sick berth attendants, wore 'fore and aft rig' – that is, conventional trousers, reefer jackets and peaked caps. We nozzers, as a further distinction, or lack of it, to set us apart from 'on-course' boys, spent our days in 'night-clothing'. It is not to be supposed that this consisted of pyjamas and dressing-gown. Throughout the Royal Navy, at least in home waters, ashore and afloat, in that quiet time after tea, at the beginning of the dog-watches, the pipe was heard: 'Hands clean into night clothing' ('clean into' was Navalese for 'change into'). The change was quickly effected; it required only the removal of the blue-jean collar and lanyard.

After we had, with some assistance, arrayed ourselves in uniform, we were ordered to change back into our civilian clothes and pack everything into our kitbags. Somewhat puzzled by this, we were led into an empty barrack-room in which stood several trestle tables. On each table were some scraps of blue serge and a can each of black and white paint. Among the kit issued to us the previous night had been a wooden die, or stamp, bearing our names and initials. Its purpose now became clear – each item of kit was to be marked with its owner's name, except the lanyard, and we had seventy-four items of kit; if you counted, as you must, a pair of socks as two items. Under the supervision of Mr Barnes and the PO, we poured paint on to the serge pads and, dipping our name-stamps in it, methodically marked every garment in the prescribed place; white on navy-blue, black on white, ranging them on the bare floor to dry. Meanwhile the PO and instructor boy, armed with steel dies and hammers, marked our boots and boot-brushes. As we worked, the gunner explained that the issue of kit we had just received was the first and last free issue of our naval careers; all replacements had to be purchased from the pusser's (purser's) store. On a warship's messdeck, he assured us, cash and valuables were safe, kit left sculling about was not; hence the need for marking. That seemed reasonable to us – what was to follow, less so.

Later, when the paint had dried, we were able at last to shed our civilian clothes and parcel them up to be posted to our homes, those of us who had one. Next morning, after cleaning stations and breakfast, assembled in the dormitory, PO Hewitt broke the news to us.

'Right. All of you – get your ussiffs out!'

Blank stares all round. The PO flourished a small roll of blue cloth above his head.

'Spelt "housewife",' he said, 'pronounced "ussiff" – get 'em out!'

We rummaged among our kit for this mysterious article. Unrolled, I saw that it contained a row of shiny new needles and bobbins of red, white and black thread. We listened with incredulity as we were told that our names were to be sewn on every last item of kit – save the kitbag, boots and brushes – and this task was to be completed before we would be allowed on course. He darkly hinted that we would be kept in the annexe until it was completed. I surveyed with dismay the kit piled on my bed, every single article emblazoned 'D.J. PHILLIPSON' in black or white paint. Full stops, the PO said, were to be included.

Of course we needed to be shown how to go about it. I can still picture PO Hewitt as we gathered round him for our first lesson. He was not everyone's idea of a sewing-mistress. He had removed his jacket to reveal a pair of indestructible pusser's issue webbing braces, his shirtsleeves were rolled up to his armpits and his much-tattooed forearms (Rule 15?) rippled with sinew as he plied with sausage-like fingers the slender needle, producing a neat chain-stitch. He showed us how to go round corners, how to knot the thread and bite it off. We were to learn that sailors are traditionally handy with a needle, whether in mending a torn sail or darning a sock. This, presumably, was the Navy's way of getting us proficient in short order; also, the task filled otherwise unoccupied periods of our days, confined as they were by quarantine. All thumbs, I made a start. The boy on the next bed to mine whistled softly as he worked his needle to spell out 'R. COX'. Such are the injustices of fate.

Quarantine did not, surprisingly, bar us from the swimming bath in the main establishment and we were marched there one morning for the swimming test. Word had somehow got around about this and, as a non-swimmer, I was apprehensive. There was a public baths in the Midlands town where I lived but during the war years, with thousands of troops stationed in the area, it more often than not displayed a sign at the door: 'HM Forces Only'. Seaside holidays were out, so the only immersion I got was on bath-night.

At the swimming-bath we were handed over to PTIs (physical training instructors), muscular, barrel-chested men with high-pitched voices. We non-swimmers, about a third of our number, were fallen-out. Having had our names carefully recorded for future attention, we were ordered up to the gallery to observe the proceedings. At the deep end, furthest from where we sat, were large wicker baskets containing suits of stiff canvas. The testees donned them and lined up in three ranks across the width of the pool. A PTI blew his whistle and the front rank entered the water, the wiser among them jumping feet first, buoyed-up for a few yards by their ballooning jackets; the show-offs executing lissom dives and surfacing with them wrapped round their heads. The Admiralty swimming test, which all boys had to pass before being drafted to sea, comprised swimming two lengths of *Ganges* full-size pool, then remaining afloat for a further three minutes in a heavy duck-suit. It was considered to be the minimum standard required of a prospective survivor. The majority passed; a handful not quite able to finish had their names taken and, much to their disgust, were sent to join the finless in the gallery. The chief PTI eyed us balefully and informed us that we were on his list of backward swimmers (a strange term to use for those of us who could not swim at all) and assured us that steps would be taken in due course to rectify the matter.

Soon after the swimming test the day of our graduation to the main establishment dawned. We had been looking forward to it, cooped up in the annexe with little variety in our lives save for cleaning duties, learning the rudiments of drill, lectures on naval terms and traditions and, of course, the everlasting sewing-on of names. Nearly blinded by needlework, stitching away long after my nearest competitor (E.W. Wilkinson) had put up his needle and thread, I still had one sock and half a mattress-cover to do, but was told I could finish it on course, before kit-inspection. Meanwhile, we could see squads of boys marching to and from instruction, swarming over the mast and drilling on the big parade ground with real rifles and bayonets and (heaven help us!) could not wait to join them.

DAILY ROUTINE

The day before we were due to transfer, lists were posted of our various destinations in the main barracks. I, and about ten others, was in Grenville Division, 19 Mess, 141 Class. Chief Petty Officer Blenkinsop, Petty Officer Lee. That afternoon an 'on-course' boy in khaki belt and gaiters (white blanco was reserved for leading and petty officer boys), in the annexe on some errand or other, called to a group of us, 'Any of you lot for Nineteen Mess?' A couple of us owned to it. 'You poor sods!', he leered, and turned away. We called to his retreating back, not unreasonably, 'Why?' He stopped and turned; we approached closer. He was a bullet-headed youth, with red face and hair and a just-about penetrable Liverpudlian accent. 'Chief Blenkinsop . . . the Black Angel, they call 'im', he said, lowering his voice, ''E's a pig's *orphan!*' With that, he marched off. My classmate and I looked at each other, and shrugged.

The following morning after breakfast, we loaded our baggage on handcarts, and after a more than usually thorough sweeping-out and scrubbing-down of our quarters ready for the next intake of nozzers, trekked up the road to the main gate of HMS *Ganges*. A particularly smart petty officer in white belt and gaiters checked us through while a Royal Marine sentry looked on impassively. We were led past the parade-ground and down the long covered way; or rather half-way down, on the left, to Nineteen Mess. Outside, in the covered way, gaitered legs planted well apart, hands behind back, head thrust forward, whole frame seemingly charged with barely suppressed ferocity, Chief Petty Officer Blenkinsop DSM watched out approach. As we came up, he growled: 'Leave that gear there, get inside!', jerking his head at the open doorway. Inside the entrance was a short corridor, or lobby, with doors opening off on either side. Ahead of us was a short flight of stone steps, on which stood a large and, in marked contrast to CPO Blenkinsop, amiable-looking petty officer. 'Boots off', he said, 'then get up here.' We removed our boots as bidden, and filed up the steps to the 'mess square'. This is a convenient point at which to describe in some detail the lay-out of a Shotley mess. First on the left inside the entrance was the washroom, a dank compartment furnished with a row of highly polished brass taps with a thick slate slab beneath, and a stack of much-chipped and dented enamel basins. Next on the left was the drying-room, a space fiercely heated by hot-water pipes double-banked round the bottom of the walls, and rows of, again, burnished brass hooks. The drying room was the only warm place anywhere in a *Ganges* mess and lingering within it was strictly forbidden. Still in the lobby, top right was the cleaning-gear store which, in the naval tradition, doubled as instructors' office and general seat of power; entry forbidden. Lastly, opposite the washroom was located the 'night-heads', locked during the day except for cleaning and captain's rounds, and available for use only between 'Pipe down' and 'Call the hands'.

Up the steps and on to the messdeck. The 'deck' itself was of parquet, with wood blocks laid in the usual herring-bone pattern. The further, dormitory section down either side of which our iron cots were ranged, bore a glassy sheen, while the lower third or so from the steps was scrubbed white as snow. This was the mess square, where meals were eaten. It was furnished with a wooden table and benches at each side, scrubbed bone-white like the floor, and a large wooden chest containing the ubiquitous tin mess-traps. The interior was distempered throughout in pale green, with a white ceiling. Between each bed was a small shelf and a casement window, latched wide open summer and winter alike. At the far end were steel racks for the stowage of kitbags and, high up under the pitched ceiling, a Tannoy speaker. Boots were not permitted anywhere on the messdeck; pusser's issue canvas slippers were worn on the mess square, stockinged feet only on the polished deck. This was holy ground; the depth of its lustre was considered indicative of a mess's moral tone and general efficiency. Even the iron feet of our cots were not permitted contact with it but rested in 'bed-chocks'; square, hollowed-out slabs of wood.

Finally, in the middle of the deck, a small coal-burning stove, black-leaded and burnished, competed ineffectually with the icy blast from the open windows.

To return to the mess square and Chief Blenkinsop. We were fallen in between the mess tables in two long ranks and answered to our names. As the last name was acknowledged a prolonged, uneasy silence descended as CPO Blenkinsop paced wordlessly to and fro before us, hands clasped behind his back, and wearing below his gaiters, we could not fail to notice, large, highly-polished, hobnail-studded boots. I shall now describe Chief Petty Officer Blenkinsop, Distinguished Service Medal, Chief Gunner's Mate.

He was a little under six feet in height, with broad shoulders and a deep barrel chest which strained his tightly buttoned uniform jacket. His arms were of more than average length, ending in large, knuckly hands, brown as teak. His face, though, was his most arresting feature. Not to use clichés like 'carved from granite', it did bear a strong likeness to those stone heads found on Easter Island some years before. He had a deeply sloping brow, large but flattish nose and a prominent lower jaw which actually protruded to reveal his lower incisors. The whites of his eyes were muddy and bloodshot, with large, sagging pouches beneath them. His complexion was swarthy, his conspicuous chin blue; his black, woolly hair lay close to his skull. He resembled, in short, a uniformed gorilla.

His stony gaze scanned our ranks as we stood rigidly 'at ease', no-one coughed or so much as blinked for fear of attracting that basilisk stare. At length he stopped pacing and turned to face us.

'Right. Listen to me. I don't say anything twice. Do I, Petty Officer Lee?' The PO grinned and shook his head in agreement.

'This messdeck is going to be your home for a long time. I am your Mother, and you will do things my way. Nineteen Mess is going to be the best mess in the Division, and that means the best in Shotley. My mess is always the smartest mess – isn't that right, Petty Officer Lee?' A slight smile and murmured agreement from our second instructor.

'You will not, repeat not, enter any other mess. You have no business in another mess. If I catch any of you hobnobbing with the offal in other messes, you will be in deep trouble – right?'

He spoke quietly in a deep, menacing, gravelly voice; the accent was modified Tyneside.

There followed a brisk, clipped recital of the daily routine here in the main establishment; a good deal more rigorous than the regime in the annexe. A lot of it seemed to consist of cleaning stations on the messdeck, though this may have been due to CPO Blenkinsop's emphasis on the subject.

'Right. Backward swimmers, prove!' ('Prove' is naval-gunnery for 'put your hand up'). A dozen or so hands, mine included, crept sheepishly up.

'When I say "prove", you get your hands up smartly, not like a bunch of fairies!' the CPO rapped, 'and keep 'em up, I want a good look at you!'

His awful gaze rested on each of our faces in turn, lingering for long seconds. 'Name?', he barked at each of us. I came to attention while keeping my right arm rigidly raised. 'Ph-Phillipson sir', I stuttered, dry-mouthed. He grunted. All of us identified, he warned us that we would have no moment of our waking hours to ourselves until we had passed the test. We would have two daily sessions at the swimming-bath; mornings before breakfast and evenings between close of instruction and supper; the whole of Saturday mornings and Friday evenings while the rest of the establishment attended the weekly film-show (he pronounced it 'fill-um') in the gymnasium. The CPO seemed to regard our lack of aquatic accomplishment as wilful. It later became clear that what was exercising him was that backward swimmers spent their Saturday mornings floundering miserably in the icy water of the baths, and were not therefore available to him for the major scrub and polish session of the week in preparation for captain's rounds.

The harangue drawing to a close, CPO Blenkinsop called out four from our ranks and lined them up before us. These, he informed us, were our leading boys, whose orders were to be obeyed as promptly as if they came from himself or Petty Officer Lee. Anyone trying it on with a duly authorized leading boy would live to regret it. None of us doubted it. I was glad to see Bob Harwood among them; we had made friends in the annexe and it seemed to me that I might need a friend in high places. If, indeed, leading boys had any friends. . . . We were dismissed and, much chastened, made our way to our respective bed-spaces and stowed our gear.

The Shotley day began with reveille at 6.15 a.m., 7.00 on Sundays. Reveille was blown on a bugle by the duty boy bugler and was known, for no ascertainable reason, as 'Charlie'. The bugle notes were followed by a tinny, disembodied voice declaiming: 'Heave-ho, heave-ho, heave-ho, lash up and stow!'

This was the traditional naval rise-and-shine formula, and referred to hammocks, with which we had not yet made acquaintance. In Nineteen Mess we would already be up and doing before reveille when Chief Blenkinsop was duty instructor, for he would rouse us at 6, as if 6.15 were not early enough on a black, icy morning, by beating with a broom-handle on the highly polished galvanized bin in which coal was kept. He did not raise his voice but stood, boots planted well apart in the middle of the polished deck, and growled menacingly:

'Out of your pits! Anyone whose feet aren't on the deck in ten seconds will go for a double on the foreshore!'

We turned out, snatched up towels, toothbrushes and pusser's-issue tin of pink, gritty toothpowder and doubled to the frigid, dimly lit washroom to grab a basin before they all got taken. There we shiveringly washed, stripped to the waist, with Chief Blenkinsop watching us from the doorway to discourage any inclined to skimp their ablutions. Some mornings there were puddles of ice on the slate slab. The precocious handful of boys who grew whiskers would contrive to shave in the evening, heating their shaving-water in a tin mug on the stove top.

Five minutes after 'Charlie' the pipe would be heard: 'Cooks to the galley'. This was the summons to collect the morning cocoa in the mess-kettle, together with a tin tray of hard-tack biscuits. The two boys who were duty cooks for the day would double off up the covered way to the galley, where they would join the queue at a vat just inside the galley door, slide the mess-kettle under the big spigot operated by the real cook, grab the biscuit ration and double off carrying the mess-kettle with its dark, foaming contents between them, to get it back while it still retained some heat. Cocoa and biscuits were consumed outside in the covered way, standing. I rarely partook; those of us already addicted would slip off to the day-heads, a brick-built block behind the messes, for a quick smoke. The cubicle doors had been removed at some time during the smoking interdiction and never replaced. An added attraction for us, still shivering from the morning sluice, were the pair of coke-burning braziers made from 40-gallon oil drums which threw out heat and acrid fumes to inhale with the Woodbine smoke. They were not supplied for the comfort of the boys at their motions, but to prevent frozen plumbing in the sub-Arctic temperature.

Ten minutes were allowed for consumption of cocoa and hard-tack before the pipe, 'Boys fall in, clean ship,' well before which we nicotine slaves had rejoined the throng in the covered way. (For the whole of our time at Shotley we each had an ear permanently cocked throughout our waking hours – and, subliminally, while sleeping – for bugle calls and pipes. There were two public clocks in *Ganges*; one on the façade of the Long Covered Way, the other in a little cupola on the roof of the sick quarters, neither visible from the boys' accommodation. We were not allowed to possess watches – Rule 7). We fell in on the mess square to be detailed for cleaning stations in and around the mess. At 7.45 a.m., 'Boys to breakfast and clean into rig of the day' was piped. 'Rig of the day' for boys under instruction was second-best uniforms, inexplicably known as 'number threes', plus webbing belt and calf-length gaiters daubed with khaki blanco in the washroom every Saturday morning and at such other times as CPO Blenkinsop deemed necessary. 'Number ones' was best uniform reserved for Sundays, special parades and long leave, distinguished by gold-wire badges in place of the workaday red worsted; in my case the insignificant AC star. Breakfast, which with other meals will be described in more detail, was a rushed affair, partaken of in night-clothing before cleaning into rig of the day.

The foregoing describes the early-morning routine of the relatively fortunate majority. Those of us who were backward swimmers donned sports rig: cotton shirt, shorts, socks and plimsolls; it was a punishable offence to wear anything under gym kit. We were despatched, shivering, to the swimming bath with the maledictions of Chief Blenkinsop ringing in our ears. Clad thus, at 6.45 on a bitter winter's morning with frozen snow underfoot and an icy wind knifing across the parade-ground to flay us when we left the shelter of the covered way, we did not loiter, but sprinted the 300 or so yards to the baths.

The PTIs were waiting to receive us, brandishing 'stonnachies', flat tubes of canvas a foot in length, filled with sand and jointed in the middle like a flail; Shotley's traditional 'liveners' for many generations. On the first morning we were greeted with:

'Chop chop, you've got two minutes to strip off and line up at the deep end!', in the high-pitched squeal affected by all PTIs.

We ran stark naked from the changing-room down the length of the pool, encouraged by stinging slaps on our buttocks, to join a score of shivering fellow-sufferers from other new classes. We donned exiguous bathing-slips and formed a ragged, apprehensive queue at a low springboard, while a PTI took up position grasping a thick wooden pole some 10 feet long. The boy at the head of the line was ordered on to the springboard, to stand at the end hugging himself, shivering with cold and fright. 'Jump!', the PTI yelped; a split-second's hesitation brought a heavy prod in the small of the back and off he went, to surface spluttering, flailing his arms, eyes wide in alarm. The pole was held out to him and as he made a grab for it, withdrawn out of reach. This sadistic procedure was repeated until, arms thrashing and having gone under several times, the lad was able to grasp the handrail at the side of the pool and cling there, coughing and retching. We each in turn underwent this ordeal by water before being lined up again on the side, dripping and blue with cold. I should mention that the water was icy at that time of morning, as the heating was not switched on until later in the day. (There was a critical shortage of coal during that dire winter, it is true, but the pool was kept at a comfortable temperature at other times of day, and we were convinced that this was deliberate policy in order to make backward swimmerhood as unpleasant as possible). If so, it was efficacious in my case; from being unable to swim a stroke, I passed the test in just three weeks.

However, there was much suffering to undergo before that happy day. On this first morning, having been half-drowned, we were relieved to be issued with kapok life-jackets from a rack on the wall and ordered to the shallow end to practise the breast-stroke for the ensuing half-hour until we were too numb to co-ordinate our limbs. I do not wish to labour the tribulations of a backward swimmer, but the foregoing account is typical; I would only add that we attended a 45-minute session twice a day, mornings before breakfast and evenings before supper, every day except Sunday.

To return to Nineteen Mess; after breakfast we cleaned into rig of the day with much last-minute buffing of boots and squaring-up of each others' collars before falling-in outside for the first of many inspections, this one by the duty instructor, and the most minute, Nineteen Mess having a reputation to make. The smallest defect – an off-centre cap-tally, a less than pristine lanyard, a smudge of blanco on a belt buckle – was enough to earn the miscreant the designation 'crabby skate' (Navy for dirty ne'er-do-well) and an extra dog-watch kit muster. We were then marched to our allotted place on the parade-ground by division, senior mess on the right, junior (us) on the left; the entire establishment paraded. This morning assembly was known at Shotley and throughout the Navy as 'Divisions'. Having dressed our ranks the duty instructor reported us 'proved and correct' to the divisional officer, who carried out his own thoroughgoing inspection, any boy with whom he found fault reporting to him at morning 'Stand easy' with the defect remedied. Inspection completed, the DO marched, with much swinging of arms, gold lace and crisp white cuffs, to the head of the parade, where waited the Commander, standing in front of the rostrum beneath the great mast; tall, silver-haired and distinguished with a telescope, his badge of office, tucked high in his left armpit. Having received Divisional Officers' reports in turn, the Commander about-faced and strode off to the 'quarterdeck', a smaller asphalt square beyond the parade-ground round which the low, redbrick administrative offices were grouped. From thence emerged the Captain, who after an exchange of courtesies with the Commander, led the way to the rostrum. As a callow sixteen-year-old my sense of the droll was as yet underdeveloped; in any case, the only perception I had of naval officers, particularly senior ones, was heavily overlaid with awe. So I missed a rare opportunity of starting the day with a smile at HMS *Ganges*.

Captain Eric Bush, DSO, DSC & Bar, Royal Navy, was a gallant old sea-dog, big in personality but small in stature; a good twelve inches shorter than his Commander. He was stocky, short in the leg and walked with a rolling sailor's gait. He had a large, craggy nose, a jaw like a ship's prow (I only saw him close-up once) and sported whiskers on his cheek-bones. The contrast with his slim, willowy second-in-command was, I am sure, quite comical. (The sardonic Petty Officer Lee obviously found it so; standing properly 'At ease' in the rear rank one morning I heard him murmur,

'Mutt an' Jeff'). The Captain mounted the rostrum to be greeted by the chaplain – *Ganges* had no fewer than three Anglicans, an RC and a visiting Nonconformist – waiting to begin our working day with a prayer and a hymn sung to the accompaniment of the Royal Marine Band. Devotions completed, we marched off in turn to the strains of 'Hearts of Oak' and dispersed to our various places of instruction. This was weekday Divisions; on Saturdays boys were occupied in 'scrubbing-out' for captain's rounds; and Sunday Divisions was a much lengthier and more ceremonial affair, with officers wearing swords and medals, a ceremonial guard mounted by the senior mess on course and followed by Divine Service in the gymnasium.

Off the parade-ground, we were re-formed into classes and doubled off to instruction in accordance with the course timetable. The morning was broken up by a ten-minute relaxation announced by the quaint pipe: 'Stand easy, place spitkids'. 'Spitkids' were metal pans the size and shape of an inverted dustbin-lid, with the inner surfaces whitewashed. They were placed outside messes in the covered ways and at the doors of instructional blocks, and intended in 1947-Shotley for the disposal of cigarette butts. As their name suggests, they were in fact Victorian naval spittoons, dating from the time when Jack Tar chewed plug tobacco, to prevent defilement of snowy holystoned decks. The end of stand-easy was signalled by: 'Out pipes. Clean out and stow away spitkids'.

A few minutes before noon instruction was 'secured' and classes doubled away to their messes for dinner. Boots were exchanged for canvas slippers in the drying-room, 'Cooks to the galley' was piped and we fell-in in two ranks outside in the covered way in charge of the leading boys, strict silence being enjoined. The food was conveyed in metal trays and fannies and dished up on to plates by the 'cooks'. We were then allowed on to the mess square and stood to the tables, opposite a laden plate. It occasionally appeared that some plates were more laden than others; if the instructor noticed this he would order everyone to move up a place (see H.J. Austin's account in Chapter 3, also for the following). The instructor then intoned in one breath: 'Any complaints say Grace. For what we are about to receive may the Lord make us truly thankful Amen.

Sit.' We then fell-to with much clattering of cutlery on metal plates, while the instructor gave us our orders for the afternoon, and any criticism and exhortation he thought due, before leaving us in the charge of the leading boys and departing for his own tot of rum and dinner.

Afternoons were devoted to sport (compulsory). We cleaned into sports rig and proceeded to the gym, swimming baths, athletics track, pierhead for sailing, or one of the numerous playing-fields abutting the establishment on two sides. Tea, a scanty meal, was at 4 p.m. At 4.30., having cleaned into night clothing, we returned to the parade-ground for 'Evening Quarters'. This was a shorter version of Divisions, without our officers or the martial sound of the Royal Marine Band who were, one hoped, in the band room practising 'Hearts of Oak'. Instead, we enacted a little choreography called 'dressing by the drum'. A boy drummer of *Ganges* bugle band marched briskly out to his appointed position midway down the parade, while we were called to attention. At a nod from the parade chief gunner's mate he beat a short rub-a-dub followed by a single *thump*, at which we simultaneously jerked our heads to the right and snapped up our right arms in line with the shoulder. At the second drum-beat we aligned ourselves, with much exaggerated shuffling of boots, with the boy next-but-one on our right. When the sound of shuffling died away the drum beat once more and we snapped our arms and heads to attention. The drummer then marched off to the foot of the mast, where he demonstrated his versatility by seizing the bugle hung on his other hip, raising it with a flourish, and sounding 'Sunset', while the White Ensign was slowly lowered. After that we marched to another hour-and-a-half of classes, followed by supper at 6.30. Our time was then our own, except for boys under punishment, to write letters, press and mend clothes or just sit on our beds reading or yarning.

At 9.15 came another quaint pipe: 'Boys clean teeth and turn in', and finally, at 9.30, 'Pipe down. Lights out', when the duty instructor extinguished the lights, save for a dim blue 'police' light at the end of the mess and ordered silence. So ended the Shotley day.

MEALS

The early post-war years were a time of austerity in Britain, with most foodstuffs still rationed, some more stringently than during the war itself. Food was very important to we Shotley boys, and though we enjoyed more generous rations than the population at large, we always seemed to be hungry. Perhaps all healthy males of our age leading a hard outdoor life have insatiable appetites; certainly we must have got enough to eat as we filled out so quickly. Our rations were adequate then, but I have to say that they were atrociously cooked.

The average naval cook, known derisively as 'slushy', or with fine irony as 'chef', was a rough-and-ready, slapdash practitioner of the culinary arts, who could be relied upon to ruin good food. Whether this was due to poor training or poor supervision and discipline, I cannot say; in *Ganges* at least all we boys saw of the galley, on our duty cook days, was the serving-hatch just inside the door. Beside it was pinned a copy of the week's menu. This varied little from one week to another; there seemed to be a limited number of dishes which were within the cooks' competence and they appeared regularly, usually on the same days of the week. Some breakfast dishes, favourites with the cook, were shown on the menu as 'HITS' (herrings in tomato sauce); 'sausages in RBG' (rich brown gravy – ha!). 'Bacon and tomato', known to us as 'tram-smash', was a flaccid, half-raw rasher swimming in watery tinned tomato. Everything that should have been fried appeared to have been steamed; perhaps this was a deficiency in galley equipment, perhaps it was just easier. Even the Sunday breakfast 'fried' egg was steam-cooked and runny. The sausages were the worst. They were actually uneatable. We were cheerful, ravenous, undiscriminating gluttons, but our stomachs rebelled at *Ganges* sausages. They came to us pale and all but raw, like the swollen fingers of a corpse, though generally likened to another part of a cadaver's anatomy by the ungrateful recipients, served in a thin brown liquid. The fact that they were always stone-cold made them no less unappetizing. The reason for this was that 'Sausages in RBG' was Saturday's breakfast, and Saturday was the day of captain's rounds. In preparation for the 'big scrub' all the mess furniture, save the beds, was dragged into the covered way as soon as we were up and washed. Winter and summer, Saturday breakfast was eaten alfresco; every mess out in the long covered way breakfasting on a slice of bread and margarine while the air was thick with flying sausages as we pelted, and were pelted by, rival messes. This minor anarchy was the nearest thing I ever saw to a mutiny at Shotley, and the instructors generally turned a blind eye as long as the disgusting gobbets were shovelled into the swill-bins afterwards. It was a scandalous waste of food in a time of national shortage, as no doubt the sausages were wholesome enough, as post-war sausages went, before the cooks got their hands on them. In the whole of my time at Shotley, I never saw a supply officer in the boys' accommodation, checking on his department's output.

Dinners were better, with plenty of stews during the cold weather, and though the meat was gristly, the dumplings leaden and the vegetables institutionally soggy, very little was left on plates. The stew was often followed by something we called 'signal-pad duff'. This was a stodgy pudding, steamed of course, mostly flour-and-water and containing a minimum of fat, and studded with raw whole apple-rings. Before being placed in the steamer the mixture was covered with sheets of paper from a naval signal-pad in lieu of greaseproof, hence the name. This paper stuck fast to the gluey mixture and was all but impossible to remove, so it generally got eaten, helped down by anaemic custard that managed to be both thin and lumpy. Our favourite 'duff', served all too rarely, was a delicious and satisfying confection called Manchester Tart. This pudding was actually baked and consisted of 'clacker' (Navy for pastry-crust), a layer of jam and cold custard set on top. If we were really in luck, dessicated coconut was sprinkled over it.

Sunday dinner, after Divisions and Church, was roast pork. The Royal Navy's Sunday dinner was always roast pork, ashore and afloat, in HM ships off Greenland's icy mountains to India's coral strand. So in later years, chewing roast pork in the steamy tropics provoked nostalgia for that bitter winter in *Ganges* (except in the Far East, where pork tasted fishy because the Chinese fed their pigs on fish-offal). Workaday tea was a slice of bread and margarine, but on Sunday we had also a piece of 'pusser's slab-cake', either fruit cake conspicuously light on fruit or dry-as-sawdust madeira. Sunday supper was always cold, usually two slices of corned beef with tinned diced beetroot and lettuce in the summer. Otherwise supper was a hot meal (or rather a cooked meal, it was seldom hot by the time we got it), consisting of a rissole or fishcake with lumpy mashed potatoes which were always flecked with brown bits, probably unremoved skin and eyes.

We took our turn as 'cook of the mess' four at a time, two from each class, for twenty-four hours. This involved, as well as collecting food when 'Cooks to the galley' was piped and dishing it up, washing up after meals, returning trays to the galley and sweeping the mess square. No extra time was allowed for these chores, so it was always a rush to be finished before the next 'fall-in' was piped. While meals were being dished up the rest of the mess was fallen-in outside, where strict silence was enforced by the leading boys. Any undue delay caused restlessness in the hungry ranks which sometimes prompted disgruntled mutterings and was a fruitful source of punishments.

'Grace' was gabbled without reverence before every meal except tea. The 'Any complaints' precursor was a ritual, not an invitation.

INSTRUCTIONAL CLASSES

Training for Boy Seamen comprised three subjects: seamanship, gunnery and schooling. Of these, the least time was devoted to the last; for AC boys one full day a week which was preceded by an evening session known grandly as 'prep'. The school part of our syllabus can be quickly disposed of; it was regarded by our instructors and – to a lesser extent perhaps – by our officers, as of little importance and so we naturally felt the same. Indeed, CPO Blenkinsop begrudged the time we spent in the schoolroom and resented our removal from his control and influence even for a few hours a week. Also, it was obvious even to us lowly boys that 'schoolies', as instructor officers were known, were very much looked down on by 'real' naval officers of the Executive Branch. A few of the former served aboard larger warships as meteorological officers and as instructors in navigation and mathematics to midshipmen, but most were employed ashore like ours, schoolmasters in uniform. They wore light blue cloth between their gold-lace stripes as distinguishing (or rather, undistinguishing) marks. Our class teachers were instructor lieutenants or sub-lieutenants, while the headmaster was a commander. There was also a full-blown instructor captain, an officer of great presence and dignity, but his function was unknown to me and the only time we boys saw him was at the gymnasium church service on Sunday mornings. He was quite elderly, and it may have been that he was retired and living nearby, donning his uniform to join us at our devotions: Captain Chips RN.

The school syllabus was confined to English, maths, geography and naval history up to, for advanced class, roughly the standard of the later GCE 'O' level. But our objective was the Navy's ET2 (Education Test Certificate Part Two), which earned us rating to Ordinary Seaman three months early, at seventeen-and-a-half. The GC class took ET1 which was little more than a literacy test.

Schooling aside, our two classes spent alternate weeks under instruction in seamanship or gunnery. There was no doubt which was preferred by Nineteen Mess. CPO Blenkinsop was our gunnery instructor; the vastly more congenial Petty Officer Lee took us for seamanship. The bulk of seamanship training, all the theory and some practical, took place in the seamanship block, a large and rambling building off the short covered way. Each of its many rooms was devoted to a particular subject – knots and splices, rigging, boatwork, anchors and cables and so on. The rooms were bare and dusty and redolent of tarred rope. There were no desks and chairs; seamanship was learned standing up or moving about. Some of the rooms contained fascinating instructional aids. In the boatwork room, for instance, were beautifully made and detailed scale models of service boats: whalers, cutters, pinnaces, gigs. There were more models in the anchors and cables room, again wonderfully detailed and exact, of battleships' forecastles, complete with miniature working capstans, tiny anchors and fathoms of Lilliputian anchor cable. On them it was possible to carry out complicated evolutions such as mooring ship, as indeed we did. These truncated battleship bows had an old-fashioned look about them, as did all the seamanship block equipment, which was apparently installed when *Ganges* opened in 1905. Little point in learning how to moor a battleship almost as the last one headed for the breaker's yard.

A sailor's basic skills are unchanging, however, and we learned some of these during our first weeks in the classroom. In the ropework room a wire jackstay was rigged along its length at chest height, with ropes' ends hung at intervals. We each took one in hand and, having watched PO Lee demonstrate, attempted simple bends and hitches: bowline, clove hitch, sheepshank, timber hitch. This was inexpressibly boring for the training-ship boys and even the ex-Boy Scouts among us, but we soon progressed to knots and splices. The splices were practical and useful; most of the knots were complicated, archaic and used mainly for ornamentation, like the Turk's Head and the Matthew Walker. I was ham-fisted and did not excel at ropework. Later in the course we were issued with hammocks – not for use until we went to sea – on the clews and lashings of which difficult and very fiddling ropework had to be carried out in our leisure time, what little we had, and presented for inspection at the twentieth-week examination. I found this task quite beyond me, despite endless demonstrations and coaching from a very patient and long-suffering training-ship boy named Wells, who in the end agreed to do mine for me for two weeks' pay, five shillings (25p).

I mentioned earlier Shotley pier and its many boats. Some were hoisted in davits on the pier itself, giving it the appearance of a passenger liner's boat deck; others were tied up to pontoons alongside. Before we were allowed afloat we had to learn the rudiments of boat-drill and how to pull an oar. An ancient, leaky cutter had been hauled up on to the foreshore for the purpose. The 32-foot Royal Navy cutter was the mainstay of *Ganges* training in boatwork; it hardly needs saying that the sailing cutter was obsolete, like the 1920s battleships and cruisers which used to carry it.

For some reason which I do not recall, Chief Blenkinsop took our class for this first lesson. It was a bitterly cold morning with a keen wind ruffling the grey waters of the estuary. We gathered round the old boat while he went through the drill in his parade-ground voice, a series of staccato barks. Each of us was detailed to a particular oar – a cutter shipped twelve and was 'double-banked', i.e. had two oarsmen to each thwart. At the order, we scrambled inboard and took up our positions. The heavy ash oars, 14 feet in length and made heavier by a sheathing of ice, lay along the gunwales. 'Out oars!', came the command. We struggled to heave the huge sweeps into the rowlocks, jabbing our neighbours in the ribs with the butt-ends and cursing silently, with much profane encouragement from our instructor. We then practised 'dry pulling', swinging more or less together, as he barked out the stroke. I was soon perspiring, despite the sub-zero temperature; the oars, blades unsupported by water, were a dead weight. At length came the order, 'Way enough!' (one further stroke and oars rested, blades horizontal). Finally, the one we were dreading: 'Toss your oars!' Chief Blenkinsop had demonstrated this movement – the trick was to brace the knee under the loom of the oar and, using it as a fulcrum, thrust down hard on the butt. As the oar swings up the other hand grips it as high as can be reached to swing it to the vertical and steady it there, blade aligned fore-and-aft. Of course it was child's play to him.

The next couple of minutes was a shambles as we struggled, grunting and sweating, to bring our oars up. Twice I got mine almost to the point of balance, only to have it 'take charge' and crash back to the gunwale, lifting me from my seat. All around, oars were thumping and flailing while CPO Blenkinsop, crouching in the sternsheets, grew angrier, making contemptuous conjectures about what we got up to in bed at night. He had unshipped the tiller (a yard-long billet of wood) and was brandishing it in a fist like a lump of teak. I had the leisure to observe this because at my third attempt, with the strength of desperation, I had managed to heft my oar erect and now rested, breathless but triumphant, the blade wobbling uncertainly far above my head, while all around me the struggle continued. The boy astern of me, a dough-faced, overweight lad named Wallace, had at last hoisted his oar up but unfortunately, having reached vertical, it kept going and crashed down on to the opposite gunwale, nearly braining his neighbour. With a bellowed obscenity, our instructor sprang forward and dealt the unfortunate Wallace a mighty crack on the head with the tiller.

Wallace was stunned, and only his cap saved him from worse injury. Having vented his fury in this manner, Chief Blenkinsop regained his self-control and by the end of the class we had more or less got the knack of tossing oars.

This incident was one of many I witnessed of an instructor striking a boy. Though officially forbidden – judicial 'cuts' being the only officially condoned form of violence – a blind eye was turned by our officers. CPO Blenkinsop was particularly given to it; his temper often got the better of him, which was a pity, because as we got to know him better – or, rather, as he got to know us – it became apparent that, buried deep beneath the formidable exterior, there flickered a spark of humanity. I recall the evening when I passed the swimming test, and returned to the mess feeling very pleased with myself. . . .

'Please sir, I've passed the test'.

'I heard', he said, 'the Chief PTI told me. Sit down and eat your supper'. 'Well done', he added. Praise, from CPO Blenkinsop! My cup was full.

'And I'll expect to see you with a fucking scrubbing-brush in your hand Saturday morning!'

On a later occasion we were having a bad time on the parade-ground. We could do nothing right and our instructor was working himself into a fine frenzy. One boy fumbled a drill movement; Blenkinsop snatched the rifle from him and grated:

'I'll show you just once more, you useless wet crow – get it right this time or you'll be doubling round the parade-ground for the rest of the morning!'

Primeval jaw out-thrust, hissing through his teeth, he demonstrated the drill movement, tossing the rifle in his huge hands as if it were a broomstick. He flung the rifle back to the hapless lad who, thoroughly demoralized, fumbled the catch and the muzzle caught him in the mouth, cutting his lip. This particular youth was really not cut out for the rigours of our existence; heaven knows what prompted him to enlist in the first place, for he was not the type to have been offered Hobson's choice by a magistrate. He was very miserable and seemed never to have got over his homesickness. Now, the tears welled up in his big round eyes and spilled to trickle down his cheeks. Chief Blenkinsop was obviously nonplussed at this;

contorting his unlovely features into what he probably imagined to be a kindly expression, he muttered:

'All right, son, all right – no call for that. Remember – the more you cry the less you piss!'

To return to the cutters. Boatwork, pulling and sailing, was an important part of seamanship training, to which most time was devoted. Apart from a few brief sessions learning how to hoist, lower and man a whaler – a type of ship's boat that was actually in everyday use in modern warships – this was accomplished by something called 'Obstacle cutters'. Each division was allocated one afternoon a week at the pierhead. Half-a-dozen cutters were manned and pulled out to line up on marker buoys out in the estuary. A starting-gun was fired at the pierhead, the oars swung and dipped, and the heavy boats were off, pulling some 200 yards to a second pair of buoys, where oars were tossed and boated, sails hoisted, and the boats were sailed round the end marker, back on the opposite tack to the midway mark where mast and sails were struck and stowed, and out oars for the final pull home. This evolution was as strenuous as it sounds; it also called for skill, strength and agility, so perhaps there was some point in cutter-drill after all. But it was some weeks before Nineteen Mess was sufficiently competent to take part in obstacle cutters; our first seamanship obstacle was the tenth week examination, due just before the end of term and Easter leave.

The examination tested our proficiency in bends and hitches, knots and splices, duties of helmsman and boxing the compass (knowing all the magnetic points of the compass: north, north by east, north-north-east etc, etc) and rule of the road at sea ('If to your starboard red appear, it is your duty to keep clear', etc), learned by rote from our individual copies of the *Admiralty Manual of Seamanship* Volume I – 'your Bible', as PO Lee impressed upon us.

This fairly elementary examination was carried out by our own Divisional Officer, Lieutenant Robson; an ex-lower decker, always the worst. I, and a few others, failed, and found ourselves, on return from Easter leave, designated backward seamen.

At least half of gunnery instruction consisted of parade training. We had learned the rudiments of drill in the annexe; now we drew battered old Lee Enfield rifles and First World War

sword-bayonets from the armoury and took to the vast, empty
parade-ground at the tender mercy of Chief Gunner's Mate
Blenkinsop. We learned to slope, shoulder, order and present
arms; how to fix and unfix bayonets, saluting at the halt and
marching – practising these drills endlessly in perishing winter
and sweltering summer; doubling wearily from end to end of the
parade-ground with our rifles held over our heads to 'buck your
fucking ideas up!' when they fell short of our instructors'
exacting standards. All this drilling did not prevent a deep and
public humiliation, when we were just a few weeks on course, for
Nineteen Mess and its gunnery instructor. The Sunday Divisions
march-past was occasionally monitored, together with the parade
chief gunner's mate, by Lieutenant Commander Wake, Shotley's
gunnery officer. He deemed our marching to be below par, and
extra backward marching classes were ordered. These took place
in the dog-watches, and it was fortunate for me that they were
done with before Easter, leaving me free to attend backward
seamanship classes. Chief Blenkinsop's mortification may be
imagined, but oddly enough he did not blame us much. Rumour
had it that he and the gunnery officer did not see eye-to-eye, and
of course rank always prevails over reputation, nowhere more so
than in the Royal Navy.

Next to parade training in importance, and even more
dreaded by us because during it Chief Blenkinsop was not
merely irascible but demented, was gun drill. This was
conducted in the battery, a vast echoing shed next to
the gymnasium. It housed, among other armaments, a twin
4-inch gun mounting. The 4-inch was a versatile weapon, used
in surface and high-angle gunnery; it was the main armament
of many wartime destroyers. We would fall-in behind
the mounting and be detailed off as gun numbers. Number one
was captain of the gun, number two gunlayer, number
three trainer, and so on. The odds-and-sods were 'ammunition
numbers', feeding dummy shells into the breech, which
was no sinecure; the guns, of course, being designed to be
fought by grown men rather than striplings, and the dummies
weighing the same as real 4-inch shells, which was quite a
lot. At intervals we would fall-out and change round, so we
all got a turn.

When it came to 4-inch gun drill, Chief Blenkinsop was in his bawling, blasphemous element, it being his favourite weapon. (He was gunner's mate in HMS *Bedouin*, a famous 'Tribal' class destroyer during the war. She was sunk on Malta convoys, the action in which he won his DSM, and he was taken prisoner by the Italians. It was our opinion that this was the real reason behind Italy's capitulation). With our instructor in this mood, sheer nerves made us muff our drill, and in a blind rage – or perhaps to simulate battle conditions – he would hurl and kick the heavy brass cartridge-cases at our feet and legs, which did little to improve our performance.

Things were a little quieter in the gunnery school classroom, where we were taught a smattering of the science of ballistics, gun-direction theory, safe handling of ammunition, and watched a number of instructional 'fill-ums'. We were examined in gunnery at the prescribed intervals by the gunnery officer and his henchmen the gunners RN. Gunnery was the only specialist subject taught at *Ganges*: torpedos, Asdic (sonar) and radar were unacknowledged.

A separate subject, of no less importance in our examinations, was physical training. This was in the hands of our old enemies the PTIs. We had two one-hour sessions a week in the gym on wall-bars, parallel bars, rope-climbing, but mostly, vaulting a box-horse: through-vault, stride-vault, long-vault and forward roll, with and without the aid of a springboard. But before any of this activity could commence (this was the PTI's favourite word of command: 'Running on the spot . . . *commence!*', delivered in a shrill squeal), we were inspected.

Our sports kit had to be spotless: shorts newly washed, with knife-edge creases, held up in lieu of a belt by a freshly laundered and ironed blue bundle handkerchief (we were each issued with two of these: they were meant to carry our belongings in, even when travelling home on leave, the Boy Seaman's equivalent of the red bandanna carried on the end of a stick by tramps in *Comic Cuts*); plimsolls spotlessly pipe-clayed. Our PTI was, confusingly, another Petty Officer Lee. We were lucky in our Lees, this one was a decent man who, while flourishing the regulation stonnachie, rarely inflicted it on us, preferring to coach rather than drive. He was short and bouncy and wore his blond, wavy, carefully brilliantined hair longer than most PTIs; he resembled a pigeon-chested Nelson Eddy.[2]

To begin with I was not very good over the box-horse. After I had, yet again, scrambled over and landed in a bundle of arms and legs on the mat, he said:

'You should see your face when you're running-up . . . you start off full of determination, then you get to about here (pointing at the spring-off mark) and you think, "Aw, fuck it!" Now go again and let's see some guts!'

I responded so well that, much later, I was only just eliminated from selection for the *Ganges* gym display team at the Ipswich fête.

Finally, the mast class. We had our first introduction to the mast during our 'nozzer' period in the annexe. We were gathered beneath it while our instructor pointed out details of the spars and rigging and demonstrated how to climb the ratlines safely. He also assured us that the large, sagging, rope-mesh safety net spread out beneath would protect the concrete from cracking should anyone lose their grip. On this first occasion we were allowed to ascend cautiously and to gain the lower platform, level with the main yard, through an aperture known as the 'lubber's hole'. We were then encouraged to climb the next set of ratlines to the upper yard, a vertiginous 120 feet from the ground. Later, during the mast class proper, this was as high as we were required to go; any further ascent up the topgallant mast, to the cross-jack or higher, was voluntary. On this first occasion, although some of our number were nervous and glad to have their feet back on *terra firma*, only one boy actually 'froze' and had to be rescued.

Mast class came round, for Nineteen Mess, every other Thursday. It was held before breakfast, in sports rig. We lined up six abreast and at the order, sprang on to the ratlines and raced up the rigging. No 'lubber's hole' for boys on course, but out along the futtock shrouds, hanging downwards like flies on the ceiling, then vertical again to the crosstrees and flying down, feet hardly touching the ratlines, against the instructor's stop-watch. Anyone taking longer than three-and-a-half minutes was sent over again, before he had got his breath back. It was just another Shotley ordeal on a bitter winter's morning with one's frozen,

1   *Mast-manning ceremony, with button boy aloft.*
(Crown Copyright/MOD)

2 HMS Ganges II, formerly the training-hulk Ganges, moored off Shotley Point c. 1910, with Harwich opposite. Note light cruiser in left background. (Crown Copyright/MOD)

3 The vast, echoing museum of Shotley's drill shed with boys in gym kit, rig of the day on sports afternoons. (Crown Copyright)

4 Shotley Open Day, 1950. Seated boys arranged on the playing-field behind the newly-built general mess hall. Signal school tower in left background, Shotley Pier right. (Crown Copyright)

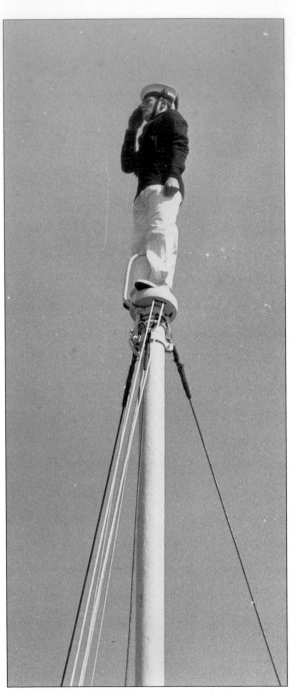

5 Close-up of button boy on his precarious perch, lightning-conductor gripped between trembling knees. It was traditional for the commander to reward the button boy on his safe descent with five shillings (25p), the equivalent of two weeks' pay.

T.S.—39.
(Revised—June, 1934.)

This card to be taken care of.

ENTRY CARD.

NAME PHILLIPSON. DAVID JULIAN

Number on Ship's Books 3351

Number of Mess

CLASS CORNWELL 2 DIVISION.   WATCH.

Instructor of Class.......... P.O. HEWITT

Warrant Officer of Division.... MR TAYLOR

Lieutenant of Division........ LIEUT MITCHELL

RULES FOR THE GUIDANCE OF BOYS.

1. On first entry, Boys are to make themselves acquainted with the Printed Orders, posted up in the Establishment for their information, a careful observation of which will prevent their getting into trouble.

2. Boys' letters are to be addressed with their Christian and Surnames in full ; their number on Ship's Books, and the number of their Mess being written on the left-hand upper corner.

3. Silence is to be kept after turning in ; and Boys are to turn out smartly when the Hands are called in the morning.

4. Prompt and unquestioning obedience to orders is essential. Talking and skylarking when on duty or when fallen in are forbidden.

N.4258/27. Sta. 50/30. Sta. 56/34.

(18/10/35) (573) Wt, 37014/8910 5M 5/36 S.E.R. Ltd. Gp. 671

OVER.

6 Entry card issued to author on joining Ganges, *7 January 1947.*

RULES.—(*Continued.*)

5. Should boys ever require any information or advice upon any subject whatever, they should go to their Instructors or to the Officers of their Division.

6. Boys are on no account to enter any of the Ship's Company's Messes.

7. Should a Boy receive any Money, Stamps, or a Money Order from his friends or wish to save his Pocket Money, he is at once to take it to the Regulating Office. He is never to retain more than Two Shillings and Sixpence in his possession.

8. Watches, articles of value, and any sum in excess of two shillings and sixpence are at once to be taken to the Regulating Office to be turned over to the Accountant Officer for safe custody.

9. Boys are prohibited from procuring Clothes, Knife-lanyards or other articles of their kit, or cigarettes and matches, either from their friends, or by purchase on shore, and all such articles found in their possession will be confiscated. Boys are not to carry knives.

10. During Leave on shore Boys are forbidden to enter Publichouses or Clothes Dealers' Shops ; they are not to lounge about or assemble in groups in the streets or pathways. They are not to trespass, but keep to the highways and public paths.

7 Extract from rules. Note deleted smoking prohibition. (Author)

8 Kit laid out for inspection. This photograph dates from the more liberal post-1956 regime, with clothing items folded rather than rolled, name-tapes in place of chain-stitch and uniform shoes as well as boots. (Crown Copyright/MOD)

9 The swimming bath. 'Backward Swimmers' spent their Saturday mornings in the icy water with swabs and cleaning-paste, removing the 'tide-mark' round the sides for captain's rounds. (Crown Copyright/MOD)

10 The author on his first home leave, Easter 1947, with shiny but hopelessly 'pusser' boots. The cap was replaced square on the head before return to Shotley. (Author)

11 HMS St James, 'Battle'-class destroyer D65, the author's first fleet ship. Note the twin 4.5-inch gun turrets and the gunnery director with flanking radar pods below the lattice mast. (Author)

12   *Author as Petty Officer aged twenty-four, sporting first long-service and good-conduct badge. (Author)*

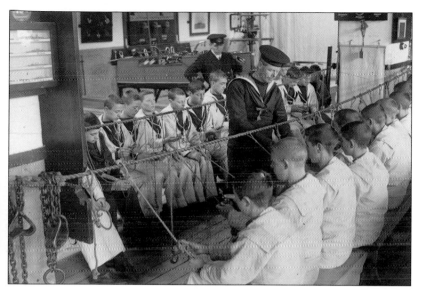

13 Boys practise bends and hitches in Ganges seamanship block. Note the battleship working model behind the commissioned boatswain-in-charge. (Imperial War Museum Q22607)

14 Ganges laundry. Boys scrubbing canvas duck-suits while instructor boy, flexing cane, looks on. (IWM Q22613)

15 Sailors in a Fight *by Thomas Stothard. A gun's crew serving one of the broadside guns while a woman tends an injured seaman. (National Maritime Museum 59/131)*

16 The Battle of Navarino *by Pierre Julien Gilbert, from an engraving by Jean Baugean. Charles M'Pherson's ship HMS* Genoa *is the right hand of a group of three in the centre background (see pp. 8–9). (NMM 59/134)*

17 Boys aloft in the sailing-brig attached to HMS St Vincent, 1891.
(NMM 59/161)

18   Small-arms drill, HMS Calliope. *(NMM 59/301)*

19   The beef screen, with cooks of messes drawing the day's issue. Royal Marine (amateur) ship's butcher surveys his handiwork while the officer of the day looks on. (NMM 59/737)

20 Industry and Oeconomy *by Henry Singleton (detail). A boy signing on for a berth at sea. (NMM 59/2159)*

21 The Main Deck of a Man of War *by T. Sutherland (detail). Jack and his doxies at play (see p. 4). (NMM A5177)*

22   *Hands washing clothes,*
HMS Marlborough, *1912.*
(NMM A4812)

23   *The daily rum issue, with 'rum bosuns' – one hand from each mess –*
gathered round, intensely interested in what the duty petty officer is telling
the supplicant sailor: probably a difference of opinion as to the number of
men 'entitled'. Note the rum tub and barricoe (see p. 145).
(NMM A8893)

24   Boys being trained in sail-handling on the 'monkey-yard' of HMS St Vincent. *(NMM A2222)*

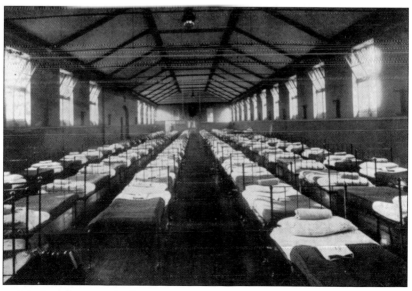

25   Royal Hospital School, Greenwich, boys' dormitory *(see pp. 31–34). (NMM P60088)*

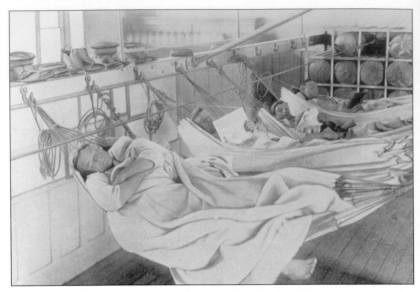

26   Jack in his hammock, where he most liked to be. This shows a barracks messdeck – note the space between hammock-hooks, also the kitbag rack. (NMM 3633)

27   Kit muster in progress, with clothing being inspected by divisional officer, midshipman and Royal Marine colour sergeant. Supply assistant (right) keeps account of discrepancies. (NMM B53)

numbed hands somehow gripping the shrouds, not feeling the pain until one was safely down. It gave us just an inkling of what the old sailormen endured, handling whipping canvas in a blizzard off Cape Horn. Mast class was perhaps less of an ordeal for me than for some others as I had a good head for heights and was pleased to find something I wasn't backward at.

DISCIPLINE

With the single exception of the decriminalization of smoking, Boy Henry Minchin (Chapter 3) would not have discerned, had he re-materialized there forty years on, any softening of discipline in HMS *Ganges*. Our waking lives, like his, were ordered and fenced about with regulation and with a prescribed punishment, individual or collective, for every infringement, great or small, so that punishment was all but impossible to avoid. The harshness of the Shotley regime did have one dubious advantage, however, as any ex-*Ganges* boy will testify; after *Ganges* nothing one later experienced was too bad.

Punishments were official and unofficial. Official punishments (applied throughout the Royal Navy) were numbered in descending order of severity. 'Number one', we understood, was hanging from the yardarm; a punishment now discontinued, like flogging round the Fleet, so there were some gaps in the scale. The commonest awarded at Shotley was 'number eleven'. This involved turning out half an hour before hands were called in the morning and mustering on the quarterdeck under the regulating petty officer. This was repeated in the dinner-hour, with an hour's 'pack-drill' in the dog-watches supervised by the duty gunner's mate, who had better things to do with his time and made his displeasure felt. Number eleven was awarded for seven, ten or fourteen days according to the gravity of the offence, or repeated offences. Inevitably, some boys were rarely off it and became 'skates' and 'crows'; like old lags outside – once in it, always in it.

A rarer punishment was number four – cells. It was usually awarded for desertion (not merely 'running') or for petty crime committed on long leave where the civil powers had handed over the miscreant to the Navy to deal with. Only the most intractable cases were consigned to cells, where half the sentence was served on 'restricted diet', i.e. bread and water, and the day was spent picking oakum under the eye of a Marine sentry. Less rare, but by no means universal, was Number 4A – 'cuts'. As described elsewhere, a caning was the assured punishment for 'doing a bunk', that is, breaking out of barracks and attempting to flee. There were perhaps a score of such cases during my time and none escaped the penalty, though there surely were mitigating circumstances in some of them. It was made known that boys trying to escape was a reflection on the Royal Navy and put the civil and military police to considerable trouble. Otherwise, cuts were awarded to a few recalcitrant cases where repeated lesser punishments had achieved no improvement. The usual number of strokes was six; twelve – sometimes inflicted in two instalments – for repeated or aggravated offences. One touch of humanity on the part of the authorities was that no punishment was entered on a boy's service record; the slate was wiped clean when a boy left Shotley, so that none began his service career under a cloud.

Unofficial punishments were frequently imposed by the instructors or even leading boys. One of Chief Blenkinsop's better points, so far as we were concerned, was that he rarely paraded a boy as a defaulter before the commander or captain. For one thing, too many boys in the punishment book gave a mess a bad name; besides, CPO Blenkinsop rightly considered himself fully capable of guiding erring footsteps on to the right path; none better. Also, there was a positive side, for those in his charge, to his fearsome reputation, and I had personal cause to be grateful for it.

The establishment was patrolled, day and night, by 'pickets' consisting of a leading patrolman (the Royal Navy equivalent of an Army redcap) accompanied by a Royal Marine, on the lookout for irregularities and infringements, however trifling. They were extremely sneaky, given to lurking in out-of-the-way corners in the hope of catching boys doing something illegal, which, as the reader will have gathered, was not difficult. Details of the offender would be solemnly entered in a notebook and in due course he would be hauled up on the quarterdeck to receive the appropriate punishment. The pickets were cordially detested by us boys for their mean and petty ways. To our surprise, instructors disliked them as much as we did. I believe there were two reasons for this: firstly, in all arms of the forces, service police are detested, and secondly, our instructors regarded the pickets' prosecution of their charges as a usurping of their own authority. Chief Blenkinsop made no secret of his contempt for them and it would have taken a bold one to set foot in Nineteen Mess, whether or not the 'Black Angel' was in the offing.

My own brush with the pickets occurred when, returning to the mess one afternoon from the gym, I lit a cigarette 'tab' in a prohibited area, namely a roadway, to be pounced upon by a picket lurking behind a coal-dump.

'Name?'

'Phillipson, sir' (To a Boy Seaman everyone was 'sir', even a Royal Marine).

'Mess?'

'Nineteen, sir.'

Royal Marine and leading patrolman exchange looks, notebook is replaced in breast pocket of tunic.

'Don't let me catch you smoking out here again. Get along out of it!'

So having a 'pig's orphan' for an instructor had its advantages.

A frequent punishment for talking after 'Pipe down' was for the entire mess to be turned out, ordered to don oilskins over pyjamas and, wearing gas-masks, to be double-marched up and down Laundry Hill, a long, steep incline running parallel to the long covered way. This exhausting, sweaty ordeal could be continued for half an hour or more. One late evening, as Nineteen Mess was undergoing this form of torment, Reverend Ambrose Weekes, *Ganges* senior chaplain, chanced by and paused to watch proceedings. 'Darby' Allen, an established skate and chancer, grasped the opportunity and, buckling at the knees, histrionically collapsed to the ground. His concerned messmates clustered round, removing his gas-mask and helping him to his feet. Mr Weekes, a short, tubby gentleman with a high complexion and big round glasses, stared meaningfully at our leading boy, an embryo-Blenkinsop named Chater, who marched us back to bed. (Mr Weekes later became Chaplain of the Fleet, responsible only to the Admiralty and the Bishop of Bath and Wells, who for some obscure hierarchical reason had pastoral care of the Navy, just as in the College of Arms, Chester Herald was the authority for ships' crests.)

We were not many weeks on course – it was about the time of the backward marching upset – when Chief Blenkinsop got us together for a long, menacing harangue on our alleged slackness. For example, in turning-out in the mornings (i.e. failed to have our feet on the deck within three seconds of Charlie's lingering last note); being filthy in our persons (performing our pre-dawn ablutions in the icy washrooms without removing our 'flannels') and spending our time in idleness (writing letters home in the dog-watches rather than studying the *Admiralty Manual of Seamanship*). He ended this tirade by threatening that if we did not buck our ideas up he would recommend the mess for Shotley Routine. If his intention was to frighten us he was successful, for we had been in the main barracks long enough to have some idea of what Shotley Routine entailed; senior messes in the Division had described it to us with ghoulish relish.

It had been devised as a 'shake-up' process for slack messes, and was a drastic measure which instructors were reluctant to take, as their own lives were considerably disrupted by it, and of course it was a reflection on their own efficiency (so a little thought should have reassured us). Shotley Routine was simply a more rigorous version of our already spartan regime, a collective punishment visited on the culpable and blameless alike. Boys were roused one hour before the rest of the establishment at 5.15 a.m., Sundays included. This hour was spent doubling up and down Faith, Hope and Charity, the Signal School's flights of steps. Mess-stools were stacked and meals were eaten standing and in silence. Fifteen minutes was allowed for dinner, ten minutes each for breakfast and supper, with tea a non-event. For the remainder of meal-breaks, the mess was double-marched round the parade-ground perimeter, rifles carried above heads. Afternoons were spent on work-parties, with no sport allowed. Kits were inspected daily. The few *Ganges* privileges – cinema shows, Shotley leave – were stopped. The day ended with a further hour on Faith, Hope and Charity. The 'dose' was two weeks, to be taken as required. No mess had ever been known to return for a second.

One crime the system was rarely required to punish was that of theft. Living as we did on top of one another, with nowhere in which to keep anything locked away, absolute trust was essential between messmates in the matter of such valuables as we were allowed to possess: cigarettes, postage stamps and money. Our weekly dole was two shillings and sixpence (12½p) rising by one semi-annual increment, on rating Boy First Class, to a maximum of three shillings (15p). It was an offence for a boy to have more than this sum in his possession; should he receive a postal order from outside, it was required to be handed in at the Regulating Office and entered to the boy's credit. There were no Winslow boys at Shotley. The authorities were well aware of the demoralization of distrust which existed in a mess with an undetected thief in its midst, and did what they could to remove temptation. Despite this, thieving did take place from time to time; not surprisingly, with a sprinkling of gaol-fodder among us. Sometimes the thief was detected by his messmates. When that happened, the light-fingered one would have wished fervently for the safety of the cell-block.

Returning to the mess one afternoon, I saw a commotion in the covered way, with a mob of boys gathered outside the entrance to one of the messes. As I approached to see what was going on, a figure staggered from the doorway. He was a strapping youth, crouching low and holding both hands to his head, from which blood ran, dripping from his ears and chin. Close behind came two boys wielding broom-handles. The crowd closed in, cutting off his escape; his pursuers bludgeoned him mercilessly on back, shoulders, head and arms, while those holding the ring contributed boots and fists. The victim sank to the ground, arms across his head, body rolled in a ball while the blows thudded home. He made no sound as his blood spread in a crimson puddle on the flagstones. How long this might have gone on and how it might have ended I cannot say; at that moment a tall figure crashed through the crowd, lashing out with studded boots right and left. The mob fell back and Chief Yeoman of Signals Parsons, white with anger, stood protectively over the huddled figure and spat at his attackers, 'Animals! Get off out of it!'

CYS Parsons was instructor to a nearby communications mess. He had but recently returned to service after a long spell of

hospital treatment and rehabilitation following three years as a
Japanese POW. He was still gaunt and painfully thin; his webbing
gaiters had had to be altered to fit his skeletal shins. He was a
quiet, kind man; I had never seen him in such a rage. No doubt
the barbarities which he and his shipmates had suffered during
those long years made this manifestation of boys' inhumanity
the more repulsive to him.

A stretcher was produced and their victim removed to the sick
bay. No-one was punished for it, and as far as I am aware no
official investigation was made. What I had witnessed sickened
me, too, and yet . . . . I had been the prey of thieves, and knew
the sick feeling of discovering that one's last cigarette or shilling
had been plundered. I felt, on balance, that such rough justice
was salutary, as I am sure the authorities did; the offence was
rarely repeated.

EXAMINATIONS

As the weeks and months passed, one of the coldest winters on
record was followed by one of the hottest summers. With each
new intake of nozzers, Nineteen Mess's parade-spot moved
nearer the right of the division. The important twenty-week
examination was looming. This marked the half-way point
in our Shotley careers and was very important, as a poor
showing could result in an individual being 'back-classed'. This
meant dropping down to the next junior class on course
and consequently an extra five-week incarceration at Shotley,
not to mention the humiliation and having strangers for
messmates. Also, instructors reserved an especially warm
welcome for cuckoos from another nest: a fate to be avoided.
My own performance was improving. I had been a backward
seaman since the ten-week examination, thanks to my
ineptitude in ropework, which deficiency had been largely
rectified by PO Lee in the course of extra evening sessions.
There were only a handful of us, for whom our seamanship
instructor gave his off-duty hours with his customary good
nature. In the silent dog-watch hours normal rules were
relaxed somewhat in the austere seamanship block. Woodbines[3]
were passed round and enjoyed, and we took care that PO Lee

never passed round his. Thanks to him, we all passed in knots and splices, bends and hitches.

Boatwork also went well enough. Classes were divided into crews and my crew went afloat from Shotley pier in a whaler, fortunately, as all the cutters were taken, with a commissioned boatswain as examiner. We each wore a number pinned to our jerseys and took a turn as coxswain, bowman, mainsheetman and so on. Coxswain was the most searching, of course; one had to steer the boat, correct a flapping luff when necessary and test one's power of command by frequently bawling orders such as 'Down slack on the tack-tackle!' which tackle (pronounced 'taykul') may already have been taut as a belly dancer's G-string, but the object was to give orders and see them obeyed. One could rely on one's mates to jump to it, as their turn was coming. After two hours or so the ordeal was over; we had all performed and been marked. Now the commissioned boatswain had the tiller – relieved as we were, no doubt – as we made passage back to the pierhead. He beguiled the time by shooting questions at us in turn about service boats in general: sailing rig, number of oars, life-saving capacity and so forth. It came to me:

'You . . . number four.'

'Yes sir.'

'When we put the tiller over, why does the boat go in the direction we're steering it?' Long silence.

'Sir?'

'Look, lad – we are now on the port tack, right? Sails are drawing nicely and we're heading for the pier, right?'

'Yes sir.'

'So?'

Met with blank incomprehension on my part, he turned to a brighter member who suggested, not too confidently, that the shape of the hull might have some influence.

'Right! We're not shaped like a fucking ditty-box, are we?'

Ropework and boatwork were the principal seamanship subjects; the rest of the examination consisted of heaving the lead, signals – Boy Seamen were required to achieve a minimum proficiency in sending and receiving semaphore and Morse, of about five words a minute – and last but by no means least, piping on a boatswain's call. This was a simple enough instrument: a thin, slightly curved silver whistle some four inches in length, rather like those 'silent' whistles which only dogs can hear. It had a bulb at the business end, with a hole in it. It was held in the hollow of the hand, the thumb along its length and the two middle fingers extended across the hole. Pitch was varied by raising and lowering these fingers while blowing. The correct grip was essential in controlling to any extent the sound emitted. An entire chapter of the *Admiralty Manual of Seamanship* Volume I was devoted to this ancient and rudimentary instrument, including pages filled with a kind of Mozartian shorthand scoring the different pipes. Some boys revealed a natural aptitude with the boatswain's call, and if they chose to, could take an examination to qualify as 'call-boys', which qualification earned extra pay of threepence weekly. A greater benefit was that call-boys wore a silver-nickel chain around their necks in place of the troublesome lanyard. The rest of us suffered horribly while they practised in the dog-watches. However, all Boy Seamen were required to be proficient in piping the simpler calls, in order to act as 'side-boys' at sea, assisting the bosun's mates in their duties as well as 'manning the side' to pipe the captain aboard and ashore, and to make routine pipes over the ship's broadcast.

The examination was conducted in a large, disused room half-full of dusty stacked furniture. A chief petty officer whom I did not recognize was seated behind a desk, a bosun's call lying on the blotter in front of him. He handed it to me and commanded,

'Pipe the side.' (This was considered an easy one; a single, drawn-out rising and falling note scored in the *Seamanship Manual* thus: ⌒⌒).

I made a hash of it, not least because the call was full of other people's spit. The CPO groaned and cast his eyes to the ceiling.

'Pipe down', he said, wearily.

This one was more difficult; two short, staccato notes followed by a warbling, thus:--〰︎⌒, which I surprised myself by performing perfectly. My breath, forced at pressure through my classmates' spittle, produced a liquid trill of which a skylark might have been proud, only louder.

'Typical!', growled the CPO, taking the call from me and noting his clipboard, 'the easiest one in the book, you're pathetic; give you one of the hardest and no trouble . . . I don't know what's wrong with you lot, I haven't heard a decent "Pipe the side" all morning'. He jerked his head towards the door. 'Away you go – send the next one in!'

I was relieved to find, when the results were out, that I had passed in boatswain's call, presumably on the strength of my 'Pipe down'. That particular chief petty officer was not, as far as we knew, on *Ganges* staff; we wondered if he was based at the Admiralty as a boatswain's call virtuoso with responsibility for maintaining standards of piping in the Navy.

The gunnery exam came next, consisting mainly of parade training and 4-inch gun drill. Our parade-work was quite advanced by this stage on course, and was considered important enough to be examined by the gunnery officer himself. With rifles and bayonets fixed, wearing our number-tags, we sloped, ordered and presented arms, marched and wheeled, marked time, about-turned, halted and ported arms for inspection, fired a make-believe *feu de joie* with empty magazines. As we sweated under a hot June sun in our thick blue serge, the ordeal ended with a complicated ballet choreographed many times by Chief Blenkinsop at his blasphemous best, known as 'From the Halt to the Halt on the Right Form Squad!', the purpose or usefulness of which in times of war was not imparted to us. On this important occasion, we all finished up in our correct positions, which was not invariably the case. Gun-drill also went without a hitch; we were examined by a boyish gunnery lieutenant with Chief Blenkinsop for once a silent onlooker, which helped, as did keeping the guns at only a few degrees of elevation to make loading easier. Our final marks were well above average, but if our instructor was gratified he was careful not to show it. Not long after the twenty-week, we all went off on three weeks' summer leave, with the heartening thought that on return, Nineteen Mess would be heading for the final stretch at Shotley Barracks.

DRAFT CLASS

The training syllabus for Boy Seamen at HMS *Ganges* comprised forty weeks of instruction, including the five weeks' nozzer time in the annexe. To this must be added seven weeks of leave and a fortnight spent in fatigue details around the barracks known as 'Work Ship', to make the total time in *Ganges* – if one escaped illness or back-classing – a little less than a year. Signal Boys, because of their wider-ranging and more technical training, served a further five months of durance vile. For seamen, the senior class on course (actually the senior mess comprising two classes, AC and GC) was known as the draft class. For its final three weeks at Shotley the draft class followed a special routine, exempt from all routine parades and musters as it prepared for final examinations and passing out.

The draft class could be easily recognized as it swaggered up and down the covered ways, seamanship or gunnery manuals in hand, at odd times of day en route to its special classes, as its members were attired all day in shabby 'night-clothing'. This was because their 'number twos', blue-jean collars and lanyards had been sponged, scrubbed, brushed and pressed as appropriate, carefully stowed in linen-bags and put away for the dreaded 'commander's kits' which took place during the last week on course. It was during this final period that boys were measured for their long-awaited 'sea suits'; so superior to the baggy, shapeless, irredeemably 'pusser' suits issued from the appropriately named 'slops' on joining. These made-to-measure 'tiddley' (Jack's word for stylish and smart) suits, while conforming to the spirit of uniform regulations, incorporated a number of subtle improvements: a fraction less width to the collar, a fraction more depth to the jumper's V-neck, which was cut to gape slightly; a snugger fit at buttocks and knee and an inch more width to the bell-bottoms. Boys could not yet afford to patronize the civilian naval tailor[4] but Shotley sea suits were the next best thing.

Final examinations followed much the same course as the twenty-week, allowing for the greater proficiency attained and some advances in the syllabus, putting a last polish on skills learned. A very high standard of physical training was demanded, especially in the gymnasium, where a gruelling examination was undergone in rope-climbing, parallel bars and vaulting. I am pleased to report that, when its turn came, 141 class was a credit to its popular PTI, Nelson Eddy. The gunnery

finals was much the same as the twenty-week except for the
inclusion of a written paper which comprised about forty
questions with multi-choice answers. In 1947, that must surely
have been a very early instance of the method. The questions
were not difficult and finding alternative answers must have
tested the ingenuity of the setters (e.g. 'How is the speed of an
enemy vessel estimated?': (a) 'By means of an instrument for
measuring the size of the enemy's bow-wave'). Always uneasy
with classroom work but determined to maintain 141 class's
high aggregate marks, Chief Blenkinsop decided to help us. En
route to the gunnery school he halted us on a dimly lit roadway
and informed us in a hoarse whisper that the commissioned
gunner would read out the questions and then the alternative
answers: a, b, c or d. He, Blenkinsop, would stand behind the
gunner and signal the correct one – nose-scratch for 'a', hand in
pocket for 'b', and so on. At our request he repeated the signal-
code, impatiently. It all went very well and we scored an average
of 95 per cent, the Black Angel being too cunning to give all
correct answers, though our papers would not have withstood
close scrutiny, so perhaps he had an understanding with the
gunner after all.

Towards the end of a boy's time at Shotley, he was allocated to a
Port Division. These were three: Devonport ('Guzz'), Portsmouth
('Pompey') and Chatham ('Chats'). Every Royal Navy warship –
with the exception of submarines and light coastal forces, which
had their own bases – was based at, maintained in and manned
from one or other of those ports, usually for the length of its active
life. A naval rating, too, spent his shore service at his port division
and his sea-time in ships manned from it. When he married he
found lodgings there, and became a 'native' (the Royal Navy trailed
well behind the British Army in provision of married quarters as in
other matters; naval quarters only became universal in the 1950s
and '60s, in time for many of them to become surplus to
requirements following defence cuts). At *Ganges*, a pretence was
made of an element of choice of port division and boys were
invited to state a preference, but when the lists went up, invariably
the Londoners and Home Counties boys were allocated to
Chatham, the Scots, Irish and Northcountrymen to Devonport,
together with the comparatively few Westcountrymen to be found

in the Navy, and the rest to Portsmouth. In this way, many close friendships forged on the anvil of HMS *Ganges* were broken, for ratings from different port divisions rarely came into contact with each other thereafter.

With a port division came also an official number, prefixed by the divisional initial D, P or C, and JX denoting Seaman Branch, thus: D/JX 819588. With Shotley's obsession with marking things, it was promptly stamped in large black letters on hammocks and kitbags. It was also entered indelibly on paybook and service history sheet and belonged to the rating for the rest of his service. A naval rating also had a quite separate ship's book number. This was much older in origin, dating to long before the Navy became a regular service, when crews were recruited or pressed for the duration of hostilities. It was allocated to a rating on joining any HM ship or shore establishment, when he was entered on the paymaster's books and became entitled to victuals and pay.

Duly numbered, and entering their final week on course, the draft class were at last issued with their sea suits, after an ultimate trying-on and adjustment in the tailor's shop. Examinations completed, the final hurdle was commander's kits, preparations for which had been going on for weeks. This legendary occurrence was too big an occasion for the messdeck, and took place in the gymnasium, to which kit, kitbags and hammocks were conveyed in a handcart. Blankets were spread upon the gym's polished deck, and an hour before inspection was due to commence laying-out began. Most items of kit had been meticulously washed, pressed, rolled and clothes-stopped days before and carefully stowed away for this moment. With kits laid out in strict accordance with the diagram in the *Seamanship Manual*, with the minutest adjustments being made to alignment of flannel vests with gym shirts, seaman's jerseys with blue bundle handkerchiefs, while instructors and divisional officers fussed worriedly about. Dead-centre at the foot of this immaculate array, its dazzling whiteness matching that of the spare cap equally exactly positioned at its head, lay the Sunday-best lanyard, 'cheesed down' in a neat flat coil. And at last something to hang on the end of it. Another extra issue made only to the draft class was 'knife, seaman's, one' (knives of any description were strictly forbidden in boys' training establishments and possession of one, even a schoolboy's pocket knife, was a 'cuts' offence – Rule 9). It was a solid, heavy clasp-knife with a broad blade and fitted with a spike for splicing; though it would equally well have removed a stone from a horse's hoof in that unlikely contingency. The seaman's knife was known to Jack as a 'pusser's dirk'. It was stamped, of course, with the owner's name.

With kits laid out to the DO's satisfaction, there was just time to double back to the mess, discard the shabby 'number threes' and clean into sea suits for a hurried inspection. Then back to the gymnasium, each boy fallen-in and standing properly 'At ease' with silence enjoined, to await the commander's arrival. We waited, shooting surreptitious glances at each other's kits, all of which looked neater than one's own. It was a traditional belief in *Ganges* that the commander picked upon a different item of kit for particular scrutiny each time he inspected; the buzz had gone round that it was oilskins for us. For once, rumour proved true.

PO Lee, stationed in the lobby as look-out, warned of the retinue's approach. The master-at-arms led the way (the commander did not rate a Marine bugler). The 'Jaunty' had a particular interest in boys' kits and not, of course, a benevolent one. He, we knew, would be searching beadily for misappropriated or unlawfully altered items ('wilful damage to Crown property'), though how the former was possible with every last piece of kit boldly marked with paint, chain-stitch or die-stamp, was unclear. But the Naval Regulating Branch seemed to have an obsession with Jack's garments and used terms borrowed from HM Customs & Excise; unmarked kit was 'contraband clothing', while that legitimately come by but bearing another's name (e.g. bought at auction of a deceased shipmate's effects) had to be stamped with a large and disfiguring black-paint circle enclosing the letters 'DC' for declared clothing, to avoid prosecution every time kits were mustered.

The commander followed, with the supply lieutenant-commander at his heels and the DO tagged along behind. The Jaunty ordered oilskins to be unstopped and shaken out, with name showing. Inspection began, each boy in turn coming to attention and stating his name which was emblazoned seventy-two times over at the commander's feet. That august being glanced down a patrician nose for a few moments at each array and passed on, without comment. The Jaunty followed, snatching up oilskins and examining them closely for dirt, tears and loose or missing buttons while fixing their owners' eyes with his own piercing stare, as if plumbing them for guilty knowledge. The procession's slow but steady progress was interrupted by a small commotion at a kit a few places down from mine. 'Taff' Woosnam was a wiry, foxy-faced Welshman and a back-classed 'skate', always in trouble. Whatever his other shortcomings however, and they were manifold, he could not be faulted on the neatness of his person and his kit. His whites were whiter, his creases sharper and his boots shinier than anything the rest of us could attain. He had had more practice than the rest of us, having been back-classed twice. We had ungrudgingly admired his kit – it will be understood that it is difficult to transform an awkwardly shaped garment with various excrescences such as collars and sleeves, into a perfectly regular, smooth and un-lumpy cylinder. We did our best. But Taff had excelled himself; his 'swiss-rolls' were perfectly formed and without blemish. Almost suspiciously so, the master-at-arms thought. He stooped, picked up a gym-shirt, squeezed it, pulled off the stops and shook it out, whereupon something fell to the deck which on closer examination proved to be a scissored-out section of one of the chaplain's hymn-cards, distributed to morning Divisions for our daily act of worship. The chaplain's yeoman, an elderly AB with no good-conduct badges and a weakness for rum, had been complaining of a mysterious deficiency of hymn-cards.

'Put this Boy Seaman in my report', the commander instructed the Jaunty, who could hardly contain himself. In the rear, Petty Officer Lee grinned his ready grin. After that, the rest of commander's kits was an anticlimax.

Final examination marks were posted and were well above average; no-one was back-classed. Chief Blenkinsop, though less than fulsome in praise, appeared satisfied, and he unbent enough, after supper on our penultimate evening in *Ganges*, to regale us with his war experiences. We gathered round him on the mess square, some of us perched on the tables, a transgression which at any other time during the previous ten months would have brought upon us a dog-watch scrub-out of the entire messdeck, and listened spellbound.

The Black Angel's destroyer, HMS *Bedouin*, was torpedoed by an Italian submarine while escorting a Malta convoy in 1942. He described the sinking: 'My Abandon Ship station was No. 5 Carley float', he told us. 'When I went to it, it wasn't there. When I looked round, I saw it'd been blown to the top of the fuckin' funnel. I 'ad to wait till the bastard ship sank to get in it.'

He did not tell us how he came to be awarded the Distinguished Service Medal.

There is little more to relate of HMS *Ganges* in 1947. There was no special passing-out parade: on our last Sunday Nineteen Mess was addressed by Captain Bush who wished us luck in our careers, and we had the honour of leading the march-past – senior mess on parade at the last. We already knew what ships we were to join: 141 class, the ACs, plus a handful of the GCs of 42 class were for HMS *Ulster*, a destroyer of the Boys' Training Flotilla based at Rosyth on the Firth of Forth. So we were not finished with training yet. The rest of the GCs were drafted to HMS *Anson*, a battleship of the Home Fleet. 'A pusser battle-wagon, loads of bullshit!', we ACs gloated, but that was before we had experienced bucketing through the Pentland Firth in a force nine gale in a narrow-gutted 2,000–ton destroyer. But I anticipate.

On a cold, grey, mid-December morning we clambered aboard our lorries and jolted past the mast and the figurehead and between Shotley's ornate gates for the last time, our departure witnessed by a bored sentry and the commander's fox-terrier, Pontius.

FIVE

Boys at Sea

The worst time of your life is when you're a boy and an
Ordinary Seaman. You expect it. When you're a boy you have
to call an Able Seaman Sir, at least you had to when I was a
kid. If he was an AB and he told you to do something you had
to do it and call him 'Sir' too.[1]

Eager as most boys were to join a sea-going ship of the Fleet,
there were disillusionments in store, some of which have been
referred to. The Boy Seaman was at everybody's beck and call; in
some ships the boys were turned out an hour before the hands to
scrub decks. He would have received a tiny increment in pay on
rating to Boy First Class but his wage was still mere pocket-
money, and meagre at that; his shore-leave was generally
restricted to a few hours on one day a week. He was frequently
caned for minor breaches of discipline as were his betters, the
junior midshipmen.

It was easier for him to offend, being left very largely to shift
for himself as the lowliest and least regarded of a ship's company
with its own problems and discontents, lacking as he now did the
continual supervision of the instructor of his training-ship days,
so irksome at the time. But then, he had to learn to stand on his
own feet, for soon enough (though even a year seemed a long
time in naval service) he would be rated Ordinary Seaman and
take his place among the men. In the early years of the century,
most of those men were remarkably little changed since the days
of sail; the ships evolved faster than the seamen. The great
spread of literacy brought about by the Education Act of 1870
had not reached the older sailors – as witnessed by Charles
Cutler, a Boy Seaman who in 1900 was recently out of training
and awaiting sea draft aboard the *Victory*, at that date used as a

receiving ship at moorings in Portsmouth harbour. She numbered among her crew many old seamen of the immovable sort later to be known as 'barrack-stanchions':

> At night times one of the crew used to come round and ask if anyone wanted any fish and chips and you paid a penny for chips and twopence for a piece of fish. He'd take your penny or twopence and go in one of the dinghies to Gosport and come off with a sack full. While he was there the old hands, all old salts with whiskers, who couldn't read or write, would gather round the galley. There, one of the younger seamen used to read to them from a novel. He'd sit on the coal bunker in the galley and these old salts would gather round and he'd read them part of this novel, how the squire's son got off with the gardener's daughter – all this tripe. They'd have their pints of beer (we had a little canteen aboard, open for an hour) and they used to give him drinks out of their beer for reading. And these old salts would sit there and wonder what had happened to the gardener's daughter when the squire's son got hold of her and this fellow used to pile it on and these old boys would sit there with their mouths open. We used to write their letters for them and read any replies back to them. They generally had the best jobs in the ship – tanky, store-keepers and Lower Deck sweepers. And all the money-making jobs.[2]

How comic this picture of simple old salts as the new century dawned, quite at home below decks in Nelson's great flagship, taking their simple pleasures – pure *Pinafore*! And what objects of scorn to the modern boy. But they were cunning and resourceful enough when it came to making some extra money against their retirement. Naval tobacco was issued in the leaf, and its processing into plug for smoking or chewing was laborious and time-consuming. As with anything on the lower deck – laundering, tailoring, boot mending – there was always someone who was willing to relieve you of the task, for a price:

> When you used to draw your pound of tobacco you're supposed to make up your own from the pound of leaf but these 'bacca firms – undercover boys – used to do that for you

for threepence. I was wiped into this crowd, being a Seaman Boy, to give a hand with this. I never got anything out of it. I simply helped to do it. And they'd have all these pounds of 'bacca with the man's names down, and out of each pound they took a quarter and made three-quarters up. They made a pound for every four for themselves, besides their threepence. They put plenty of canvas round and plenty of thick spun yarn to make it look a nice big perique of 'bacca. All the spare pounds they used to make up and take them ashore and sell them to the dockyard men. They used to get 1s 6d a pound for them, or something like that. That was one of the swindles.[3]

Baynham states that the introduction of manufactured tobacco soon afterwards put an end to this illicit trade, which is true, but leaf tobacco continued to be issued as an optional take-up for another fifty years and was processed in the traditional way, as the author has many times witnessed. In a Home Fleet destroyer in 1949, there took place a monthly 'soap and tobacco' issue. When it fell due a form was circulated to messes by the Stores Petty Officer ('Jack Dusty') on which all ratings, boys included, made their requests for issue. On offer was a half-pound tin of cigarette tobacco (known as 'tickler', after the famous makers of tinned jam), or a half-pound tin of manufactured pipe tobacco, or three-quarters of a pound of loose leaf and (for the really economically minded, when proprietary brands of soap-powder were available in the ship's canteen) up to two pounds of 'pusser's hard' (see Chapter 4). There is a reason for the leaf allowance being apparently more generous than the other, and it is this: the stalk from each individual leaf had to be carefully removed and all stalk and trimmings returned to Stores where it was weighed and landed to the Victualling Yard under the supervision of HM Customs; it would be ground down to make snuff. Four ounces of stalk was required to be returned from the twelve ounces of leaf drawn.

There were a couple of dozen boys aboard the destroyer referred to, occupying the boys' messdeck aft. They were provided with a sea-daddy, to supervise their cleaning and cooking duties, in the shape of a wrinkled, taciturn three-badge AB ('Stripey') who was one of the handful who drew their tobacco allowance in this form. Stripey's method of constructing his perique (pronounced 'prick') of tobacco will interest the reader as it did his young charges, who watched the process with fascination.

Having carefully trimmed the leaf of stalk and put it aside, Stripey smoothed each leaf flat one on top of another to form a wad which was placed on a rectangle of flannel cut from a discarded seaman's vest. He would then sprinkle the wad liberally with grog from his tot, hoarded for this purpose, after which it was rolled up in the flannel and taken to a length of spun-yarn (loose-laid, tarred line) tied to an overhead hammock-bar. The end of spun-yarn was knotted round one end of the parcel and then tightly rolled all along its length, Stripey leaning back with all his weight on each turn until the perique was lashed snug and taut from end to end, when the yarn was cut and tied off. After two weeks or so the perique was unlashed and cut with a razor-sharp penknife into thin, dark, richly smelling discs, to be rubbed between horny palms into a loose shag for smoking as required.

By this date, there was no longer a demand for periques of tobacco among dockyard 'maties', but there was a ready market for 'tickler' at ten shillings (50p) for a half-pound tin. This was where most pusser's tobacco went. Naval personnel enjoyed remarkably generous duty-free privileges while United Kingdom-based which the other two services did not, and this gave rise unsurprisingly to much jealousy on the latter's part. The reasons are historical and need not concern us here: suffice to say that this was one of the few hang-overs from the Navy's past that worked to Jack's advantage. And to that of his officers, with their duty-free wardroom gin, which was why any rating caught smuggling and thereby putting this privilege at risk, was dealt with harshly – disrating with consequent loss of pay and pension in the case of petty officers and leading hands and cell punishment for junior ratings; this for a first offence. Smuggling went on nonetheless. Much of the pusser's issue was trafficked rather than smoked because ratings, boys included, were able to buy virtually unlimited quantities of cigarettes from the ship's NAAFI canteen at duty-free prices, so only a few economically minded sailors bothered to hand-roll 'ticklers'. Cigarettes were specially packed for naval use; both packets and individual cigarettes bore the legend 'HM Ships Only'. There were other, secret, differences to help Customs identify them as contraband when found in the wrong hands.

The daily rum issue was the other lower deck 'perk', though boys had not been included in this since the 1840s. In the modern Navy, young seamen were also excluded until they were twenty. Every rating on joining a ship was issued with a 'station card' bearing his name, rate, ship's book number, watch (port or starboard) and part of watch (first or second), and whether he was 'G' (grog), 'T' (temperance) or 'UA' (under age). It was rare indeed for an entitled man not to draw his grog for, even if he did not wish to drink it himself, it was valuable currency and could buy almost any service. Chiefs and petty officers drew their half-gill tots neat, while junior ratings' grog was diluted with two parts water. The size of the daily tot had been successively reduced since the middle of the nineteenth century (half a gill is equivalent to a public-house treble) and was finally abolished on 31 July 1970, after 240 years. The reason given by the Board of Admiralty was that 'in the light of the conditions of the modern Navy the rum issue is no longer compatible with the high standards of efficiency required now that the individual's tasks in ships are concerned with complex and often delicate machinery and systems, on the correct functioning of which people's lives may depend'. This certainly applied to technical ratings, whose proportions rose steadily in post-war years, but the dab-toe sailor, scrubbing paintwork or leaning on his broom, must have felt pretty glum about it.

Before 1970 then, the newly drafted boy had his rating to Ordinary Seaman to look forward to a year or so ahead and, not long after, his first tot. He had probably tasted rum before that; adult ratings sometimes bestowed 'sippers' or 'gulpers' from their tots on favoured boy chums; a practice which was strictly illegal. The morality of officialdom providing a daily dose of strong drink to mere youths might have been open to question, and may have been at least partly the true reason for ending the tradition in a more enlightened era; certainly a few alcoholics were launched on their careers because of it and, equally certainly, the vast majority took no harm, just as in society at large.

In the past, rum – too much or not enough of it – had been

the cause of much indiscipline and discontent, and even mutiny on more than one occasion. A case is recorded in 1794 when the crew of the *Defiance*, 74 guns, lying in Leith Roads, mutinied because their captain had ordered the men's grog to be watered by five parts rather than the usual three (the ration at that time was one gill served twice daily). It was winter, and the men complained that the spirit so watered was 'thin as muslin, and quite unfit to keep out the cold'. The mutiny ended only when another 74-gun ship was brought alongside with guns primed.

Fortunately for Boy Seamen, it was an unwritten rule that they should never be actively involved in mutiny; this was a man's affair, because of its dire consequences. Boy Bertram Kiel was serving in HMS *Leviathan*, flagship of the Fourth Cruiser Squadron, part of the Mediterranean Fleet in 1911:

> We had been out on the firing ranges off Morocco, on our way back to Gibraltar, and it was six o'clock before they piped tea. On our way into harbour the Commander gave the order to holystone the decks – and we were going to coal the next day. There had been no time in the period between coming from Morocco to holystone the decks or anything, so they slung the sand down, but the Officer of the Day went and reported to the Commander that they had simply sprinkled the sand down and never used the holystone. The Commander piped 'Clear Lower Deck. Everybody aft.' Of course the lads got to know what it was all about, so only a few of the leading hands and the POs and all the boys went aft. All the Seamen were at the screen doors. So the Commander got the Master-at-Arms and two of the Marines . . . and ordered them under close arrest for joining in a mutiny. Two or three of them flew at him and struck him . . . and so he jumped on top of the capstan so they couldn't get at him. It didn't finish until between twelve and one o'clock in the morning and we boys were kept on the quarter-deck witnessing all this.[4]

The biggest and potentially most dangerous mutiny of the twentieth century took place at Invergordon on the Cromarty Firth in September 1931, when the Atlantic Fleet exploded in full-blown mutiny over proposed pay cuts. The Invergordon

Mutiny, which had serious repercussions abroad and is said to have been the chief cause of forcing Britain off the gold standard was, not uniquely, the result of ignorance and insensitivity on the part of politicians towards the first and arguably the most important of Jack's alleged three preoccupations: Pay, Prick and Pud. The mutiny lasted for five anarchic days and has been much written about elsewhere but again, there is no record of boys taking an active part. Where men refused duty, the boys, together with the petty officers and most of the Marines, seem to have mustered as ordered or, as in the battleship *Rodney*, stayed below in their hammocks and out of harm's way on the 'advice' of the seamen.

In all other circumstances boys serving in ships of the Fleet played their full part in working, and in time of war, fighting their ships. Boys were frequent casualties in both world wars: reference was made earlier to Jackie Cornwell VC and his messmates in HMS *Chester* who were killed; youths of sixteen to eighteen, whose presence at and participation in a great and bloody sea battle was not considered in any way remarkable. The Army, on the other hand, considered boys of that age too young to fight in front-line trenches (though some did, having falsified their ages on enlistment) for which the minimum age officially was eighteen. In the Second World War, Boy Signalman Briggs was one of only three survivors when the battle-cruiser *Hood* was blown up by a plummeting shell from the *Bismarck* in the Denmark Strait in May 1941. There were other, less famous boy-survivors, and some who died.

With the surrender of Germany and Japan and the end of hostilities, the size of the Royal Navy was vastly and rapidly reduced. Older ships were sold or scrapped; others were reduced to reserve or, in the uneasy international situation of the time, 'cocooned' or 'moth-balled' against future need. The rump remaining in active commission was much restricted by post-war economies in consumption of fuel oil and spares. But in spite of this massive rundown the Navy still had urgent manpower requirements because it was demobilizing tens of thousands of hostilities only ratings and time-expired continuous service men whose release had been delayed by the war: the situation was, in fact, very similar to that experienced at the end of the Napoleonic

Wars referred to earlier. The problem was compounded by a sudden decision by the Labour Government in 1946 to reduce National Service from eighteen months to twelve. The Home Fleet was at one period reduced to a single cruiser and four destroyers because of overseas commitments, while other ships were left with only nucleus crews.

With recruitment and training a high priority however, resources were found to maintain a Boys' Training Flotilla consisting of three wartime Fleet destroyers, based at Rosyth on the Firth of Forth. It was to one of these that the author, together with the rest of 141 class, travelled from Shotley Barracks in mid-December 1947.

TRAINING FLOTILLA

To our delight, Petty Officer Lee was drafted with us. Chief Blenkinsop, having made his gruff farewells and actually shaking hands with some of us, had packed his own kitbag and departed to be a recruiter in his native Tyneside. We received this news with incredulity. I remembered the kindly old CPO who had so disarmingly engineered my own bondage and tried to imagine Blenkinsop leering at some innocent young Geordie while handing him a pen and jabbing an enormous finger at the dotted line. . . .

An interminable journey in a succession of those dirty, cold, clanking post-war trains found us at last rumbling over the Forth Bridge to Inverkeithing railway station, whence we marched a mile and a half through a steady drizzle in sodden greatcoats and with gas-masks slung, pushing handcarts piled high with kitbags and hammocks, to the dockyard where our ship for the next three months, HMS *Ulster*, lay alongside. Nearby up the quay were moored her sister-ships *Wakeful* (flotilla leader) and *Wrangler*.

We had seen a warship's messdeck only once before, and briefly at that – during a day's cruise aboard HMS *Cowdray*, a small 'Hunt' class destroyer, mid-way through our Shotley course. The boys' messdeck in *Ulster* was aft, down a hatchway opening on to the after-flat, or alleyway, where the boys' heads and bathroom were located. We clattered down a steel ladder into a warm and brightly lit rectangular space with cream-painted bulkheads and deckhead, cramped enough with thirty boys and their kit in it. There were three 'broadside' messes; two athwartships on the starboard side, the third aligned fore-and-aft opposite, each furnished with a wooden table, two long mess-stools and shelves for tin-gear. Around the bulkheads were ranged steel lockers with red rexine cushions covering their lids, the only colour on the mess-deck, which doubled as extra seats. Close under the deckhead, around and between the bowl-shaped light fittings, ran a Clapham Junction of 'channel plates'; shallow, perforated metal trays which carried electrical wiring around the ship. Also beneath the deckhead, on either side, stretched the 'punkah-louvers', ventilation trunks fitted at intervals with adjustable 'blister' openings, similar to those found nowadays in passenger aircraft cabins and motor-coaches. The overhead furnishings were completed by hammock bars fitted across the width of the messdeck 10 feet apart.

The spare space next to the port-side mess was filled by the hammock 'nettings', in fact a barred enclosure like a Brobdingnagian play-pen, and steel kitbag racks. The deck was covered in corticene, a thick and highly durable mud-brown linoleum.

Ulster's messdeck is here described in some detail because the description applies exactly to every junior rates' messdeck in every ship in the Royal Navy during that period. The last surviving example may be viewed aboard the museum-ship HMS *Belfast*, 6-inch cruiser, now at permanent moorings on the Thames at Southwark.

In the forward corner of the messdeck, behind a curtain under the ladder, was a small enclosed mess occupied by our instructors, PO Lee and the gunner's mate Petty Officer O'Kane, who spoke pure cockney, having sold his birthright for a mess of jellied eels. We were twice lucky; 'Paddy' O'Kane was a nice man, strict but fair, and humorous.

PO Lee called over our names and allocated us to one of the three messes; ten or eleven in each. It was now after 10 o'clock and supper-time was long past; we had left *Ganges* at seven that morning and we were more tired than hungry in spite of having subsisted all day on railway tea and a bag-meal comprising an 'oggie' (Cornish pasty) containing a dry and tasteless, largely vegetable filling encased in 'clacker' of a jaw-breaking density, an apple, an orange, and a leaden slab of pusser's fruit-cake. Nevertheless, while we were slinging our hammocks the instructors appeared with a mess-kettle of the immutable ship's cocoa, steaming hot and sweetened, for once; loaves and margarine were uncovered in the bread bins to supply a sparse repast. The POs supervised our turning-in: some hammock clews needed adjustment to avoid tipping the occupant out. We had never slept in hammocks before and found them surprisingly comfortable, and in spite of our unfamiliar surroundings, soon lost consciousness.

We were roused at 6.30 by the shrilling of a bosun's call and the traditional exhortation of 'Heave-ho, heave-ho, lash up and stow! Rise and shine, the morning's fine' (this was a formula, not a weather report: in three winter months in Scotland, fine mornings were rare as the smile on a parade gunner). Petty Officer Lee moved among the hammocks, jabbing at the tardy, and supervised our lashing-up. A hammock is tightly lashed with seven equidistant turns of the lashing. It has of course to be done while still hanging, for the lashing must be hauled taut with all one's weight at each turn, having first arranged the mattress and blanket into a neat cylinder within. It took some time and several attempts for most of us before our instructor was satisfied and we could lower our hammocks and stow them neatly upright in the nettings. Then to the bathroom to jostle for one of the eight hand-basins – stainless steel and fixed, not chipped enamel and stacked loose, as at Shotley. The water was hot and there were two showers, but no time for that.

Ulster, we were informed, was 'under sailing orders'. This applied to any warship which was putting to sea within twenty-four hours, and was a warning to libertymen that if they went 'adrift' (i.e. late in returning from leave) and thereby missed the ship, they would be deemed absent without leave until they were able to rejoin, which might not be for several days, and punished accordingly. This stricture did not apply to us boys as we were allowed liberty only, as at *Ganges*, for a few hours on Sunday afternoons. Sunday afternoon in a small Scottish town in winter – once was generally enough.

Our first breakfast aboard *Ulster* was kippers and marmalade, and we ate ravenously (I was to taste that succulent kipper a second time, but that is to anticipate . . .). *Ulster*'s ship's company used the 'canteen messing' system, where each individual mess did its own catering and food preparation. Meals for boys under training, however, were prepared and cooked by the galley staff. Again as at Shotley, all we had to do as 'cook of the mess' was to collect the food, dish it out and wash up afterwards. Under each mess-table was a noisome galvanized pail, known as a 'gash-bucket', into which food scraps and slops were emptied. 'Gash' is Navalese for spare, surplus, unwanted. Washing up was done at the end of the mess-table after it had been cleared, in the mess-kettle, a versatile utensil which also conveyed soup, porridge, cocoa and any other more-or-less liquid comestible except tea, which was brewed in a tall, cylindrical metal vessel incorporating a strainer for the leaves. For washing-up, the mess-kettle was filled with hot water from the bathroom, in which was agitated a perforated tickler tin containing a few scraps of pusser's hard, in a usually vain attempt to work up some suds. The cook's last job was to take the gash-bucket and mess-kettle up on deck and empty their contents down the gash-chute, a steel trunking which hung over the ship's side, invariably attended by a raucous gang of seagulls fighting each other for scraps. The ditching could also be accompanied, if the cook had been careless, by a metallic *clink* as an item of cutlery was consigned to the deep along with the washing-up water. This was a serious matter and, if it happened often enough, a mess might be reduced to eating with its fingers or using a bent cigarette-tin-lid as a spoon; this could and did occur, as a full set of mess-traps was issued on a ship's commissioning and not replaced, unless lost through enemy action. Hence the lower deck litany: 'Tinkle, tinkle, little spoon; knife and fork will follow soon.'

After breakfast on that first morning we were ordered up top to fall-in on the quarterdeck to be introduced to and inspected by our divisional officers. We had been divided into two divisions: Forecastle (pronounced 'folksul') and Quarterdeck: I found myself in the latter. My DO was Lieutenant Roberts, tall and slim with a quiet manner and somewhat sardonic, disillusioned smile; Lieutenant Hughes, young, boyish and enthusiastic, had the Forecastle. We split into our respective divisions and our instructors took us on a tour of the upper deck; starting on the fo'c'stle with its capstan and cables and working aft by way of a 4.7-inch gun mounting, the wheelhouse with its ship's wheel, gyro-compass repeater and engine-room telegraphs; down the waist past the four torpedo tubes and the motor-boat and whaler snugged-in on their davits; finally aft again to the quarterdeck to examine the depth-charges in their racks and throwers. Various sailors working about the upper deck ignored us, in a friendly way.

As our tour ended, a bosun's call shrilled 'Stand easy'. We rushed as one boy to the NAAFI canteen situated in the forrard flat and formed a noisy queue at the serving-hatch, until ordered to 'Cut the cackle, you fuckin' sprogs!' by a wizened individual in a singlet and *déshabillé* boiler-suit with its sleeves knotted round his waist, who was trying to make himself heard ordering eggs and a jar of pickle. We had other purchases in mind: cigarettes at ninepence (4p) for a packet of twenty, and bars of 'nutty' (Navy for any sort of confectionery, whether or not containing nuts). Before half of us had been served the call 'Out pipes' was heard and the canteen hatch was slid shut, leaving the rest to get their supplies at dinner-time. For the nicotine addicts among us cigarettes at such a price were an unimaginable boon: since the 1947 Budget which abolished duty-free privileges in shore establishments, cigarettes at Shotley's canteen had cost 2s 3d (11p) for twenty; almost a week's pay. 'Nutty' was rationed on board, and vouchers were issued monthly, but the allowance was much more generous than civilians enjoyed, and in any case, 'nutty tickets' could usually be scrounged from adult ratings who had lost youth's sweet tooth.

After stand-easy, we were ordered to clean into overalls and fall in on the jetty, to assist in storing ship. *Ulster* was to depart for Scapa Flow at 4 p.m. We were excited at the prospect of putting to sea; had we been even slightly more seasoned, the humming of a gusty north-west wind in the signal-halliards would have warned us of what was in store. Blissfully ignorant, we turned-to with a will on storing, forming a human chain between the piles of provisions dumped on the quayside by dockyard lorries to the upper deck forward for striking below; spaced out across the quay, up the brow (gang plank) and along the deck, passing sacks of potatoes, onions, cabbages, sides of bacon and cases of condensed milk and, under the beady, narrowed eyes of the Officer of the Day and Jack Dusty, several wicker-bound stone jars of Nelson's blood. At 11 a.m. 'Up spirits' was piped (Jack's version – 'Up spirits – stand fast the Holy Ghost'), at 11.50 a.m., 'Cooks to the galley. Hands of messes for rum', and at noon, 'Hands to dinner'. No rum for us of course, and dinner was a thick slab each of fatty beef with boiled potatoes, cabbage and gravy. When the pudding appeared, a resounding ironic cheer went up – it was our old friend, signal-pad duff. After our exertions of the forenoon, however, little was left over for the gash-chute. At 1.15, 'Hands fall in, work ship' was piped – at least, that is what PO Lee told us the pipe was, as he chivvied us off the messdeck to fall in, forrard or aft as appropriate. We soon got to know the routine pipes and could recognize the tune, so to speak, if not the words: two of *Ulster's* four bosun's mates were Glaswegians, with the impenetrable, to Sassenach ears, accent of that city of culture. It always seemed that the least comprehensible in any ship's company were given the job, rather like railway announcers.

Our division fell in on the quarterdeck to be detailed off by the killick, Leading Seaman 'Jasper' James, a dashing character with hawk-like features and a curly black beard. Leading hands were so called from the killick, or small anchor, worn as a badge of rank on the left sleeve. He issued half-a-dozen of us with buckets, scrubbers and soft soap and set us to washing paintwork; the first few square yards, had we known it, of many acres of paintwork to be scrubbed down by us until we became killicks ourselves and dished out the cleaning-gear. Half-way through the afternoon a ten-minute stand easy was piped, just long enough for a smoke, squatting inside the screen door out of the biting wind.

At 3.30 the pipe came 'Hands secure for sea' and, dirty weather being anticipated, we were put to lashing loose gear and fitting wire strops to secure the depth-charges in their racks; then, at 3.45, by which time we had been sent below to clean out of overalls and into number threes, 'Special sea dutymen to your stations'. This was the order for the yeoman of signals and his 'bunting-tossers' to close up on the flagdeck behind the bridge; the Coxswain (a chief petty officer, the equivalent of master-at-arms in a big ship) and his quartermasters to take the wheel and man the engine-room telegraphs; a lookout to double forrard to 'the eyes of the ship' and the lifebuoy-sentry aft to the quarterdeck. Hand-cranked telephones wailed and alarm gongs rattled as communications were tested. With all the practice Shotley had given us in shifting rigs at speed, we were on our way up top when 'Hands fall in for leaving harbour' was piped. We were fallen-in on the port side of the quarterdeck, facing inboard and standing at ease; the ship's company quarterdeckmen were likewise arrayed to starboard. Lieutenant Roberts arrived and took up his position right aft, under the ensign-staff; Jasper called us to attention and reported 'correct'. The order came to 'Single up', which meant to cast off and reel-in extra mooring-wires, leaving just the stern rope and the back-spring to let go when ordered. This evolution was carried out smartly at the run by the quarterdeckmen as we looked on, prevented from getting in their way. Faintly on the gusting wind we heard the tinkle of the engine telegraphs and felt a vibration under our feet. At 4 p.m. precisely came the order 'Let go aft' as the ship juddered into life and water erupted and foamed under our stern. We were called to attention and about-turned to face outboard as *Ulster* slipped away from the quay, leaving the heavy pontoons which had kept us off the wall bucking and tugging at their bridles in our wash.

With just steerage-way on, we slid past *Wakeful* and *Wrangler* and, in the courteous naval tradition, saluted them as we did so. Bosun's calls sounded the 'Still' (in a big ship this would have been 'one G' from the marine bugler), hands lining the guardrails were called to attention, our captain and officers on the bridge faced *Wakeful* and saluted as our Ensign was dipped. *Wakeful* and *Wrangler* responded in kind as we put on a few knots and pointed our bows to the dock entrance. We remained fallen-in until we had passed into the Firth and under its mighty bridge, a fish's-eye view making it look even more colossal than seen from shore, with *Ulster*'s masthead seeming just to scrape under the massive central span. Once clear, we were dismissed with the pipe, 'Special sea dutymen secure, first dog-watchmen on watch. Hands to tea and shift into night clothing' ('Secure' is Navalese for pack up now).

An explanation which may be needed is that the naval day at sea is divided into seven 'watches', commencing with the Afternoon watch from noon to 4 p.m.; First Dog, 4 p.m. to 6 p.m. and Last Dog (not Second) from 6 p.m. to 8 p.m., followed by the First, Middle and Morning of four hours each until 8 a.m. and finally, the Forenoon watch until noon. The two-hour dog-watches create an odd number of watches so that a ship's company divided into two or four for watchkeeping enjoy a rotation of duties and in the latter case, 'all night in' every fourth night. Boys however, excused the rum ration, were also excused watchkeeping, and we went below for tea.

This meal consisted of tea brewed in the tea-fanny with tinned condensed milk added, bread and margarine, and jam. The jam, bright purplish-red and sweet but with no discernible flavour, issued on a daily basis, along with sugar and margarine from Jack Dusty's store, arrived as a large, ladle-shaped dollop in the middle of a dinner-plate. Tea was eaten as we steamed down the Firth towards the open sea. Bulkheads creaked as *Ulster* lifted a little to the swell, and the more susceptible of us began to look thoughtful. After tea, the instructors emerged from their own mess and showed us how to secure (in its general sense) loose gear against rolling. Gash-buckets were lashed to a table-leg; mess stools laid on their sides on the deck; tin-gear wedged into the mess kettle, this in turn being tied to a stanchion. Afterwards, left to our own devices, most of us went on deck to experience the unfamiliar sensation of being on a ship at sea and also, as the unsettling motion increased, to satisfy a need for fresh air. Up top, the air was very fresh, with a stiff, cold breeze from which we sought shelter on the lee side of the after superstructure. The night was pitch-dark so there was little to see but our tumbling, foaming wake illuminated by the stern-light attached to the ensign-staff bracket. Just visible was a necklace of twinkling lights on the distant shore-line, and on our port beam a lighthouse flared its brief warning and flicked into darkness again.

A whiff of acrid funnel-fumes made me feel queasy and, shivering, I went below. A few hammocks were already slung, their occupants having given up the struggle. Later, when supper appeared and proved to be liver and boiled potatoes, I slung mine and turned in. There followed a few anxious minutes as I lay there swaying, swallowing copious amounts of saliva and calculating the distance to the gash-bucket, before sleep intervened. I was jerked into consciousness several times during the night as *Ulster's* by now violent motion caused me to bump, and be bumped by, neighbouring hammocks, separated by only the regulation eighteen inches space per man, or boy; also by the mess-deck Tannoy crackling into life at intervals with quietly spoken orders for change of watches, without the shrill piping, as a thoughtful concession to the slumbering mess-decks. The piping resumed at 6.30 however, with a call we boys could not ignore: 'Call the hands, call the hands – Heave ho, heave-ho, lash up and stow', etc. PO Lee appeared, with the customary grin on his round, red face, to turn us out and oversee hammock stowage and morning ablutions. As sleep wore off, nausea again churned our stomachs and breakfast was far from our thoughts, but our instructor made us eat, if only dry bread. 'You'll feel better for it', he said. We didn't. The tea-fanny swung giddily at the foot of the table, suspended from a hammock bar on a length of cod-line. Few of us partook.

We dressed in caps, boots and overalls, and on the pipe 'Hands fall in, clean ship', went on deck to be detailed-off by Jasper. The duty cooks of messes stayed below to scrub out; we did not envy them. On the way up we enountered a bosun's mate in the after-flat, who informed us cheerfully that it was 'blowin' a bastard up there'. That seemed a fair description of the conditions – a grey dawn and a full gale in the Pentland Firth; that notorious stretch of water with its lumpy, confused seas even in gentler weather was a sight to behold for us 'sprogs'. As we grabbed at anything handy for support, including each other, the stern rose and fell with an almost corkscrewing motion and green seas boiled inboard. The watch on deck had rigged life-lines fore and aft; wire jackstays with ropes'-ends dangling from them, so that one progressed like strap-hangers on the Tube. It was clear that no work could be done on deck, and Jasper James ordered us back into the shelter of the after-flat and allocated jobs, mostly the eternal washing of paintwork and polishing of brass with 'Bluebell' and chunks of cotton-waste.

Myself and another, however, were sent forrard to report to the petty officers' mess, for a purpose unspecified. Having knocked timidly on the bulkhead beside the baize curtain screening this Olympian abode and been bidden to enter, the PO's messman, another stripey, handed us a knife each and a bucket of potatoes and told us to get peeling. The motion here, under the fo'c'stle, was even worse than down aft, and on the third potato my head swam, my protesting stomach heaved, my mouth filled with saliva and I suddenly could not bear the smell and slimy feel of raw potato. I dropped everything and fled on deck, just making the ship's side in time to 'muster my kit'. I clung tightly to the guardrail as I did so, as if life still had some meaning. On eventually raising my head I saw that I was not alone, but had joined a short file of crew members, one of them a PO, similarly occupied. That made me feel a little better, as did voiding the contents of my stomach, for I had at last got rid of the taste of that oily breakfast kipper of the previous day, the rancid tang of which kept arriving in little burps ever since I had begun to feel unwell. After gulping fresh air for a few moments longer, my *Ganges* training asserted itself and drove me back to my place of duty.

When the messman was satisfied with our output and released us, we returned aft along the raised catwalks, clinging to the life-lines, our feet alternately leaving the deck as the ship fell away beneath them, then surging upwards again, bending our knees like Groucho Marx's. Beneath the scudding clouds and spume-filled air, the white horses raced at us from every quarter, hurling *Ulster* about like a dinghy. Delivery was at hand, however. Jasper, in dripping oilskins and spray-spangled beard, flung out an arm towards a low-lying smudge of land just visible off our starboard bow. 'There she is, lads – Scapa!' (pronounced 'Scapper', not 'Scarper' as the Cockneys have it). Scapa Flow was the great Fleet anchorage in the southern Orkneys loved or loathed – mostly the latter – by the matelots of two world wars. Now, at the end of 1947, it was all but abandoned by the Navy.

By late morning and 'Up spirits' (so appropriate!) we were in the lee of the island of Hoy, shaping-up at reduced knots for Switha Sound and the old destroyer base of Lyness. *Ulster*'s wild motion subsided, life-lines and sea-lashings were unrigged, cooks of messes went below again and peeled spuds for dinner. Lyness was a huddle of hutments and a half-dozen cylindrical oil tanks, framed against the low, hump-backed hills of Hoy island. As we carefully closed the long wooden jetty a small group of figures approached to take our lines. Some wore Afrika-Korps ski-caps, others grey-green leather jackets and trousers; all had large orange discs sewn on their backs and knees. 'Fuckin' Jerries!', someone said. There was no armed guard with rifle and fixed bayonet (where would they run to?); a big man in a long, black leather coat gave them orders.

We spent two days at Lyness, during which the gale abated, though the wind remained brisk. Non-duty watch boys were granted shore leave, to wander around the all-but-deserted ghost town of the once-busy, crowded base with its huge, locked cinema and small, still-functioning wet canteen, entry to which was forbidden to boys. I was fortunate on the second day to be detailed to go in the motorboat to Kirkwall, the capital, to purchase crates of fresh eggs for the wardroom. My function was to lift and carry; the motor boat was coxswained by a tubby two-badge AB and the leading steward brought the cash and conducted negotiations at the little grocery store. But it was an interesting trip, chug-chugging cautiously between rocky islets, on the edges of which scores of seals basked – if basked is the right word beneath steel-grey skies with a cold breeze whipping spray up the rocks. On the way back to *Ulster*, with a quite lively popple in the Flow, I sat in the stern-sheets with my feet braced against the egg-crates to prevent movement.

Having taken fuel, during the forenoon of the third day we sailed, back to Rosyth but performing various exercises and evolutions on passage. The boys had their own seaboat's crew. The 'seaboat' was always the ship's whaler, so-called because in this mode it could be, and was, launched in the open sea, while the ship was under way. The procedure was as follows: when the pipe was heard 'Away seaboat's crew, watch on deck lower seaboat' those of us in the crew raced to the starboard waist where the whaler hung in its davits. (Should the pipe be 'Away *life*boat's crew', it was manned by whoever was nearest, including the chief cook if he was one of them, for it meant a man was overboard – same boat, different designation). While the watchmen were knocking-off the gripes and turning the davits outboard, we scrambled up the jacob's ladders into the boat and set about preparing for launch. A whaler rigged as a seaboat was 'set-up' on a patent quick-release gear, where the whole weight of boat and crew was taken up on chain slings which could be released by a small lever close to the stroke oar's hand. The captain went to the bridge, releasing the officer of the watch to go on deck to take charge of the launch. The whaler was lowered to within a few feet of the waterline: all depended on the skill and judgement of the OOW who, ideally, timed his order 'Slip!' to drop us on a wave-crest, rather than, with a spine-jarring crash, into a trough. Even so, the robust but narrow-gutted whaler leapt and skittered about alarmingly, still tethered to its parent by the thick, springy coir boat-rope until the bowman let go, while the rest struggled to ship their oars and pull away from the looming ship's side before being bounced against it. The situation in a seaboat on launching, especially into a choppy sea, was one, as may be imagined, of frantic if well-drilled activity and not a little controlled panic. The procedure was always watched by an audience of 'guardrail critics'; oily stokers and pimply stores assistants who didn't know a poppet from a gudgeon–pin but were free with advice. Usually during these drills, the lifebuoy-sentry stationed on the quarterdeck was ordered to hurl a lifebuoy over the stern: this was deemed to be a man overboard and we would pull away to retrieve it while *Ulster* hove-to and turned broadside to the sea to provide a lee for re-hoisting. This was a similar procedure in reverse: the disengaging gear was set up again on the way back, the whaler manoeuvred under the 'falls', or hoisting-tackles, and hooked on. 'Clear lower deck' was always piped for hoisting the seaboat, which meant all but watchkeepers manned the falls. No sissy devices like winches.

When slack was taken up on the falls so that the boat was half out of the water, six heavy rope lifelines were tossed over the ship's side, one for each of the crew. The coxswain and bowman stood fast in the boat; the other four shinned like monkeys up the freely hanging lifelines to deck level, where waiting hands grabbed and pulled them inboard. We saw the point, now, of those hours and hours of rope-climbing in the Shotley gym. The boat was then jerkily hoisted by about eighty pairs of hands and stamping feet, wooden fall-blocks creaking and squealing. When at last the falls were 'two blocks', the OOW bawled 'High enough!' and while the hands on deck took the weight, bowman and coxswain passed *their* lifelines up and over, round and round the blocks forrard and aft respectively, and leaned back on the loose ends. The order 'Ease to the lifelines' was then given, the hands backed up a little and, if the lifelines had been properly passed, the blocks eased apart until the whole weight of the whaler was on the two lifelines. This enabled the disengaging gear and slings to be hooked on, ready for the next launch. If the lifeline failed, allowing the boat to slip, the boy responsible was at the worst overboard and at the best, on captain's defaulters and a month of backward seamanship classes.

'Away seaboat's crew' was practised daily when *Ulster* was at sea; sometimes more than once. All boys took part, and we each had a turn at coxswain. It will be appreciated that a very high standard of seamanship was called for in getting the whaler safely away, often in high seas, pulling a mile or more to retrieve a barely visible lifebuoy from the grey waste and returning to the controlled chaos of re-hoisting, with its potential for injury or worse. And these were not grown men; the eldest was sixteen and three-quarters. It was not courage or bravado which allowed us to perform these prodigies, but discipline – the *Ganges* brand of it, fear of the consequences.

In fact, the only injury sustained during our three months took place on an occasion when I had the ill-luck to be coxswain. The incident occurred some weeks later, when *Ulster* was returning from exercise in company with *Wakeful*, the flotilla leader. The flotilla surgeon had been signalled aboard *Ulster* to treat one of our stokers who had fallen down a hatchway and dislocated a shoulder. When he was ready to return, the doctor was prevailed upon to board the whaler at the davits, this presenting yet another opportunity to exercise the seaboat which had not been lowered for a full two days. We scrambled up into the boat.

The MO was a young surgeon-lieutenant RNVR doing his National Service; a red-haired Scot, small, slightly built and dapper in his sparkling new uniform. He seemed ill at ease, gingerly seating himself on the stern-bench as I hurriedly checked the gear, inserted the wooden bilge-plug, shipped the tiller and reported to the officer of the watch:

'Ready in the boat sir!'

The watch on deck lowered away. *Ulster* rolled lazily in the deepish swell.

'Slip!' roared the officer of the watch.

The stroke oarsman jerked the lever and we fell a good seven feet into an inopportune trough as the OOW misjudged it. The doctor and I, gripping the edge of the stern-bench for dear life, just managed to keep our seats as the crew were flung to the bottom-boards in a tangle of limbs, oars and boathooks. We rose on the next crest to the level of the wildly swinging fall blocks. We, an experienced seaboat's crew, ducked; the MO, an LRCS, did not. Before I could shout a warning, the heavy block caught him a blow on the forehead which might have been very serious had not the brunt of it been taken by the shiny peak of his new uniform cap. As it was, he sustained an inch-long gash which bled freely.

I was in something of a quandary. The crew had sorted themselves out and were pulling strongly away from the ship, as they were trained to do. Beside me, meanwhile, a valuable naval officer was white-faced and seemingly leaking his life's-blood into the bilges. I glanced back to *Ulster*'s quarterdeck, where a group of figures were gathered: officers, petty officers, side-boys, the chief bosun's mate and, I believe, the chaplain. Most of them were gesturing and shouting things which I could not hear. This was where my training took over – 'Always obey the last order' was dinned into us from our first day at Shotley. My orders were to deliver the doctor to his ship, which I proceeded to do.

The crew were pulling with a will towards *Wakeful*, lying hove-to 400 yards away. The MO was pressing a folded handkerchief to his brow to staunch the bleeding and irritably refused my offer of first-aid from the bag at his feet. We drew alongside *Wakeful*'s accommodation-ladder; I gave the order 'Way enough', the crew boated their oars and the bowman plied his boathook to hold us in. We bucked to the swell as our passenger rose unsteadily to his feet to disembark. As naval protocol required, I raised my right arm smartly in salute as the officer stepped over the gunwhale, while presuming to extend my left to his elbow in support. At that instant a sudden lurch caused him to throw out a hand which descended squarely on my cap and, off-balance, I sat down heavily on the stern-sheets. Muttering an un-Hippocratic oath, the MO climbed thankfully, I was sure, to the safety of *Wakeful's* deck. Her officer of the watch, who had eyed these proceedings inscrutably, greeted his bleeding brother-officer with a salute and dismissed us in the courteous naval manner: 'Thank you, coxswain. Carry on please.'

We returned gladly to our ship. After hoisting, I was ordered to report to the first lieutenant, who questioned me about the incident. No blame was attached to me for the mishap; as, indeed, none was due, my boat drill for once having been faultless. I denied having heard any order to return to *Ulster's* gangway. We did hear subsequently that *Wakeful's* commanding officer, Captain (D), had remarked on the inadvisability of committing ships' officers into the care of juvenile boats' crews. We also heard that *Ulster's* wardroom were amused at the thought of the MO's wound being sutured by his own petty officer sick berth attendant; an inept and sadistic boil-lancer whose ministrations were to be avoided unless *in extremis*.

'Away seaboat' was by no means the only evolution practised on *Ulster's* training cruises off those Scottish coasts and islands though, as has been indicated, it was the most frequent: this was because it was the cheapest. No oil fuel was burned; no mechanical parts worn out. It was expensive only in manpower, of which there was no shortage in an HM ship ready at all times for war. We were also drilled on one of *Ulster's* 4.7-inch guns, under the Gunner's Mate, PO Paddy O'Kane. The drill was pretty much the same as for Chief Blenkinsop's beloved 4-inch, except that the ammunition was separate; that is, there was a steel projectile and a cordite cartridge which were placed in the loading-tray and rammed into the breech by hauling with all one's strength on a steel-wire lanyard. Any boy whose strength proved wanting received the customary Gunnery Branch slurs about leaving it alone at night. The 4.7 when fired made an earsplitting bang and clang which reverberated round the confines of the gun-shield, and in our heads for the rest of the day. Not that it happened often; in fact we only fired live once, and were allowed two rounds of ammunition; in other drills we merely pretended to pull the trigger. Likewise our go at depth-charge firing, with only one charge dropped. This produced a spectacular muffled explosion and a great eruption of water high in the air. As it subsided a few assorted fish floated belly-up on the surface: the seaboat was piped away to retrieve them.

Next to seaboat, we practised most the duties of helmsman. Half a dozen of us at a time crowded into the wheelhouse and took turns on the wheel and telegraphs, with our divisional officer looking on. The officer of the watch on the bridge above would give a succession of helm and engine orders down the voicepipe, as might be:

Boy (prodded by DO): Boy Jones on the wheel sir.

OOW: Very good. Port fifteen.

Boy (spinning wheel smartly to the left until the brass pointer behind the wheel shows 15): Fifteen of port wheel on sir.

OOW: Ease to five.

Boy: Ease to five . . . five of port wheel on sir.

OOW: Midships. Steady.

Boy (returning wheel to midships and reading course off gyro-compass repeater at eye-level): Wheel's amidships sir. Course one zero nine degrees.

OOW: Very good. Steer one, one, zero.

And so on.

There was no more schoolwork for us now; most of us had passed the ET2 for advanced rating before leaving *Ganges*. In the long gaps between training cruises, lying on the jetty in Rosyth Dockyard, we were sometimes marched ashore to a cold, dirty hut and lectured on gunnery and torpedoes. I recall a session on small-arms conducted by Paddy O'Kane. He was demonstrating how to handle the Webley service revolver, a very heavy, cumbersome and wildly inaccurate weapon. It was not a live demonstration, of course, but quite thrilling; Paddy had served on the old China Station before the war, and showed us the famous Shanghai Crouch. With a grim expression on his blunt, square-jawed features, he gripped the revolver in both fists and bent his knees. This reduced the target area presented to an assailant, he informed us. Hunkered down thus, hands pointing the gun fully extended in front of him, he sprang into the air and landed facing 90° to his left, then to the front, then to the right and finally, to the front again and straighten up. This was an effective counter to being attacked by crazed Chinese from all directions, presumably in a crowded opium-den. It was not braggadocio on Paddy's part which prompted the demonstration, but a good-humoured response to our pleading.

Most of our time in harbour was spent in turning-to with the hands on work about the upper deck, or below, scrubbing-out messdecks, flats, bathrooms and heads. The latter was much preferred in the bitter winter weather prevailing, but only cooks of messes and a handful of others were so employed. The rest of us spent wearisome hours between stand-easies on the cold, tedious chore of chipping paintwork with hammers. All warships in commission, between refits, unless on flag-showing duties or ready for admiral's inspection, were dotted with patches of red lead like German measles. There were a group of seamen, the 'side party', under the chief bosun's mate, whose job was to continuously go around the ship's side between deck-level and waterline, touching-up patches of rust. Their task was never-ending, like the famed painters of the Forth Bridge whom we observed when entering or leaving harbour, spider-men crawling on the massive girders.

On one morning at least, we were virtually all employed below-decks. Saturday was captain's rounds day, as at Shotley; as, indeed, throughout the Navy. The same hurried, perfunctory breakfast; the same stripping-down and thorough scrubbing of the messdeck, polishing brass scuttles (portholes), pipe-claying canvas-covered stanchions, burnishing cutlery and mess-traps. The same making oneself scarce during rounds, more difficult in the narrow confines of *Ulster* than it had been at Shotley; dodging the procession round the upper deck and crowding into the canteen flat once it had moved aft. Not the least unpopular thing about Saturdays was dinner – always corned beef and boiled spuds, the cooks in the galley also preparing for inspection and having no time for more complicated fare. But Saturday afternoon was always a 'make-and-mend', which meant slinging hammocks and 'crashing swedes' for the ship's company; compulsory sports for us boys, a miserable couple of hours on the muddy, windswept playing-fields of Rosyth or Invergordon.

We may have had less use of our hammocks than our seniors, but we still had to ship clean ones every fortnight, when our divisional officers would inspect them. We were issued with two hammocks, and the dirty one needed scrubbing with a hard brush (the Navy's scrubbing brushes were manufactured in HM Prisons, in those days when convicts had to work for their keep) and pusser's hard soap. This took most of the fortnight to accomplish, with one small bathroom among forty boys. The hammock was spread flat on the deck, buckets of water sloshed over, the bar of soap rubbed well into the stiff canvas and followed by vigorous scrubbing to remove the grime. It was usual to work with an 'oppo', helping each other. If the ship was at sea, so much the better, as hammocks could then be bent securely to a heaving-line and towed astern for an hour or so in the dog-watches, when the first lieutenant was less likely to notice; this imparted the extra whiteness housewives dream of. Then it only required the chief stoker's acquiescence, by no means to be taken for granted, to hang them to dry above the boiler-room. From time to time also, if the weather was fine, which was rarely enough, 'Hands air bedding' would be piped. At this, hammocks would be pulled open and mattresses and blankets extracted, taken on deck and hung on guardrails and jackstays for the day. This was very necessary, as bedding soon became damp and frowsty on crowded messdecks, being tightly rolled and lashed immediately after being vacated.

In common with most warships *Ulster* enjoyed the services of a 'dhobi firm'. This was an informal partnership of two oppos who, for a consideration, took in their shipmates' washing – not 'smalls' but large and awkward items like hammocks and blankets. However, they charged sixpence (2½p) for a hammock; not unreasonable, but beyond the reach of most boys. There was another service we gladly availed ourselves of. Though hair had to be kept short and neatly trimmed, haircuts in the Fleet at large were not of the penitentiary style imposed in *Ganges*. They were really no more drastic than the popular civilian style of short back-and-sides one's father, uncles and elder brothers favoured. 'Jan' Crouch, Leading Torpedoman, plied his clippers every evening after supper in his storeroom, or 'caboose', under the fo'c'stle. He too charged sixpence but for boys, generously reduced his tariff to fourpence. This we were glad to pay to retain most of our crowning glory, especially if Long Leave was in the offing. We had been sent on Christmas Leave within a couple of weeks of joining *Ulster*. We had looked more like real sailors this time, in our 'tiddly' sea suits, buckled shoes instead of Shotley-issue boots, caps tipped well forward and cap-ribbons adorned with HMS *Ulster* in gold wire in place of the hated *Ganges* which everyone seemed to 'know' was a stone frigate for juveniles of dubious character. But we still clutched our bag-meals and blue bundle handkerchiefs; tucked into mine a half-pound tin of tickler for my father, who had faithfully kept me supplied with Woodbines throughout my Shotley time.

As our three-month course in the Training Flotilla drew to its close we had Easter Leave to look forward to; but before that, more examinations.

These occupied the whole of a hectic week in late March, part in harbour, part at sea. I must have been a late developer, surprising myself (and others) in seamanship by coming second only to an ex-training-ship boy, Don Pearce, whose favourite sport was sailing. I scored top marks in gunnery, which I loathed, having developed a remarkable power of command. 'Power of command' was an attribute highly rated by the Gunnery Branch; it was the ability to bawl orders very loudly and with seeming confidence. 'Seeming' was the operative word in my case; it helped, of course, to be bawling orders to an ex-*Ganges* squad or an ex-*Ganges* gun-crew, when instant and well-drilled obedience could be counted on. Anyhow, I blush to report that it won me the prize for the most promising boy on course. It is more than likely that the sardonic Lieutenant Roberts saw through me, for my prize was a copy of Stephen Potter's *Gamesmanship*, recently published to become a best-seller.

With passing out came a parting of the ways; the ending for many of us of close friendships formed in the trials and tribulations of *Ganges* and since. We were to be drafted to ships of our respective port divisions. A list was posted and I was pleased to discover that I was among a dozen or so allocated to HMS *St James*, a modern 'Battle' class destroyer based at Devonport, near Plymouth.

JOINING THE FLEET

On the day of departure, with kitbags and hammocks piled beside the gangway, we were issued with travel documents and despatched at intervals. We of the Plymouth contingent left Rosyth Dockyard in mid-afternoon by Royal Navy lorry and arrived at our destination, Devonport Barracks, late on the following evening. In the course of this journey from the north to the south-west of the British Isles, we made seemingly endless changes of trains. Rosyth to North Queensferry, to Edinburgh, to King's Cross, to Paddington for Plymouth and finally, Devonport. At each change, hammocks and kitbags were dragged by us (porters not deigning to handle Jack's baggage) from the luggage van, loaded on to trolleys, trundled to the departure platform and re-stowed for the next leg of the journey. At King's Cross we received the first and only assistance from the authorities in the form of a lorry to convey our kit to Paddington while we went by Underground. Arriving at last at Plymouth North Road in mid-evening, and disappointed in our expectation of naval transport to meet us, there followed another scramble to retrieve our baggage before it was carried on to Penzance, and transfer it to a little puffer to the Barracks station at Devonport a mile or so distant. There at last stood our transport: a rank of two-wheeled treck carts painted battleship-grey and bearing the legend 'RNB DEVONPORT No. 3', etc. They were in the charge of a grizzled and disgruntled AB from the barracks' baggage-party, who had obviously not taken kindly to this late turn-out for a parcel of 'sprogs'. Under his caustic direction we wearily loaded our belongings and trudged the few hundred yards of public road to the floodlit main gates of HMS *Drake*, Royal Naval Barracks Devonport. There we were fallen-in, roll called, travel documents surrendered, and given into the charge of a leading seaman who marched us through the dark and slumbering barracks to a dank, dilapidated wooden hut near the foreshore which was to be our messdeck. It was barely furnished with iron cots and a few rickety wooden lockers. However, apparently clean and dry blankets and pillows were also provided and we were ready enough to turn in after our interminable journey and glad not to have to sling our hammocks, which were filthy and stank of railway fish-boxes.

Next morning we were roused by our 'hooky' at the sybaritic hour of 7 a.m. He, Leading Seaman Harris, informed us that our ship, *St James*, was at sea on exercises and was not due back for ten days, during which interval we would be accommodated in RNB. He marched us to breakfast in the vast junior ratings' dining hall, and marched us back to the hut afterwards. 'Chats' Harris, who was obviously embarrassed by his role of nanny, explained that Royal Naval Barracks was geared to the reception and housing of adult ratings between sea-drafts; there were no facilities for boys. We would be kept in a kind of quarantine, segregated from the sailors (Rule 6 again). We would be allowed to visit the dry canteen and the barracks cinema, but only as an organized party in his charge. If one went, we all went. It gradually dawned upon us, in the teeth of our disbelief, that the powers-that-be were intent on ignoring our presence in the establishment. There was nothing for us to do – no musters, no training-classes, no working-parties apart from keeping our hut clean. There was no shore-leave either, but what we had never had we didn't miss. After our recent exertions, we revelled in idleness; reading, writing letters and wandering about the foreshore and the limited area of the barracks which was in bounds. 'For Chrissake look as if you're doin' something', admonished Chats Harris. For ex-Shotley boys, this was second nature.

Devonport Barracks was known to the matelot the world over – and to several generations, having been built in the same decade as Shotley – as 'Jago's Mansions'. The Mansions part was self-evident; the two enormous barrack blocks resembled, strictly from the outside, an Osbert Lancaster drawing of a stately home. 'Jago' was Adolph Jago, a Swiss restaurateur who, sometime in the early 1900s, had been employed by the British Admiralty as a catering advisor, again lagging behind the War Office which had retained Alexis Soyer in a similar capacity fifty years earlier. Jago was the onlie begetter of the general messing system which was first instituted in Devonport Barracks, eventually overcoming naval conservatism to replace, in shore establishments and big ships, the inefficient and much-abused 'canteen messing'. Thus a foreigner, native of a small land-locked country with neither experience of nor interest in the nutritional requirements of seafarers, made his reputation in, of all unlikely places, the Royal Naval Barracks Devonport; his memory revered on the lower deck more than Nelson's, whatever the 'Hearts of Oak' school of naval officers liked to think.

The novelty of idleness soon wore off and we were nearly as glad to join our ship when she at last returned to harbour as Chats Harris was to see the back of us. He helped us load our kitbags and hammocks on to the inescapable handcarts, wished us luck and returned gratefully to the anonymity of the depot working party. We trundled without regret through the connecting gate between RNB and the dockyard. Axles squealing and iron-shod wheels rumbling over the cobblestones, we rounded a corner and there she lay, HMS *St James*, our first draft.

She was moored alongside the jetty in the inner basin, and was a sight to behold in the early spring sunshine. The 'Battles' were beautiful ships, perhaps the handsomest of all destroyers, the sleek greyhound lines of which make them the most aesthetically pleasing of warships, though light-cruisermen might take issue with that claim. The 'Battle' class were, in any case, almost light cruisers, with their 2,500 tons displacement and twin 4.5-inch guns mounted in miniature turrets fore and aft. *St James* also had the reputation, so we had heard, of being the 'tiddliest' ship in the Home Fleet. It was easy to believe as we surveyed her gleaming paintwork, sparkling brass and dazzlingly white canvas screens. We were by now not green enough to wonder who kept them in that condition.

We propped our humble conveyances at the foot of the after gangway, a rough, unadorned structure of wood and iron painted in 'crabfat' – dockyard dark grey. We knew better than to approach the forrard gangway, embellished with chromium-plated stanchions, ship's crests and elaborately worked rope handrails; that was the front, as distinct from the tradesmen's, entrance. We humped our baggage up the gangway and piled it on deck, under the incurious eyes of the upper-deck hands stowing berthing wires and tidying up, still in their number threes from entering harbour. No-one seemed to be interested in our arrival and we were discussing whether we should seek someone out to report to, when a voice hailed us:

''Lo there, kiddoes!'

This informal greeting was our 'welcome aboard' from Petty Officer Doherty, Boys' Instructor. He came down the deck towards us, his face deeply tanned and showing signs of wear. It was a boxer's face: lean cheeks, broken nose, scarred brows a bare inch below the widow's peak of his hairline; hard, jutting jaw. His pale blue eyes were narrow and slanted which, together with his curiously shuffling gait, gave him an almost oriental appearance. His lean frame was clad in an immaculately clean and pressed boiler-suit (seaman's working-rig in 1948); blancoed 'dabs' (plimsolls) on his feet with canteen socks, which is to say no socks, and peaked cap pushed to the back of his close-cropped head.

'Oh k-k-kay kiddoes, grab yer kit, c-c'mon below.'

We followed him down the steep galvanized ladder to the boys' messdeck, dragging our kit behind us. The messdeck needs no describing: it was identical to the one we had lately vacated in *Ulster*. We stacked our hammocks in the nettings and found an empty locker each in which to stow our gear. As we did so, the messdeck Tannoy crackled into life with a thin piping and a drawn-out 'Staaand easy!', coinciding with the clatter of feet on the ladder. In no time the cramped space was full of our new messmates and a hubbub of conversation, much of it ribald. The air soon became hazy with cigarette smoke as ticklers and 'tailormades' were lit up. Tea-fannies appeared at the ends of tables.

'Better grab yerself a cup', said a mournful-looking, heavily acned youth across the table, 'there's not enough to go round.' He was right, there weren't. We sat, unrefreshed and ignored, in a corner. Later, we were to realize that there was no tradition on the lower deck of polite introductions. You joined a mess and 'made your number' or not, as you chose; in either case the initiative was with the newcomer.

Ten minutes later, the Tannoy again: 'Out pipes. Hands turn-to.' To my surprise, being fresh from boys' training where commands are obeyed on the instant, nobody moved for a full two minutes, when a shout was heard from the flat above: 'Come on then, you heard the pipe, clear the messdeck!'

'Get it off yer back, Slinger!'

'Roll on your pension, you old bastard!'

These disrespectful sallies were addressed to 'Slinger' Woods, a wizened three-badge Able Seaman who, we gathered, was Mick Doherty's deputy and aide in nurturing *St James'* boys. Despite the insolence, the messdeck quickly emptied. 'Slinger' descended and introduced himself. He invited us to partake of the rapidly cooling dregs of tea, which we did gratefully from stained, used cups. Slinger told us what we already knew, that cups were always in short supply due to breakages in rough weather and no replacements.

'That bleedin' Jack Dusty', he muttered hoarsely, 'tight as a mouse's ear 'ole. You'd think 'e 'ad to buy the bastards.' He piled the dirty cups in the mess-kettle and disappeared up the ladder with them, muttering to himself.

'Below! Right, k-kiddoes, c'mon up top!'

Mick Doherty was waiting for us in the after-flat.

'Right! Square yourselves off. You're g-gonna meet the boys' DO, Lieutenant M-Mark Mandeville f-fuckin' hyphen Cheyney. C'mon.'

We followed him along the main deck, up the ladder at the break of the fo'c'stle and through the door into the wardroom flat. He removed his cap, tucked it under his arm, and rapped on a cabin door.

'Ye-ers?' drawled a voice from within.

'S-sorr, new draft of boys, sorr', Mick reported.

'Ah – splendid. Splendid.' (I had noticed that this was the naval officer's all-purpose adjective, except when annoyed.)

Lieutenant The Honourable Mark Mandeville-Cheyney whisked aside his cabin curtain and ran his eyes over us, lined-up in the alleyway. He was tall and slender and aristocratically languid. He gazed at each of us in turn and said: 'Welcome aboard. You fellows are very fortunate to be joining this ship's company, are they not, Petty Officer Doherty?'

Mick made no reply to this presumably hypothetical question, and Lt Mandeville-Cheyney continued: 'This is a ship with a reputation, as you may be aware. We demand a high standard of our people and I have no doubt that you will be a credit to HMS *St James*. We shall see that you are.' He consulted the draft-chit which Mick handed him: 'Phillipson, Salkeld, stand fast. Carry on, Petty Officer Doherty.' Mick chivvied the rest away, while Pete Salkeld and I wondered why we were singled out. It was vouchsafed to us – in a remarkable regression two centuries back – that we were to be officers' servants.

Because of the manpower shortage referred to earlier, trained Boy Seamen were often employed to fill adult billets: this was the case in *St James*, which was at that time losing several of her ship's company every week to demobilization. A significant proportion of the upper-deck hands – forecastle, maintop and quarterdeck – were boys, as were the gunner's and boatswain's parties. It was explained to Pete and me, however, that the duty of officer's servant was voluntary and we could refuse it if we chose. Neither of us had any principled objection to what sounded like a 'quiet number' and, in any case, we had never been given the option before to refuse anything, and it was all too much for us. Having indicated our willingness, Lieutenant Cheyney informed me that I was to be his servant, and sent Pete off to report to the gunnery officer, his new master. Initiation into my new post began at once with a lightning tour of my officer's wardrobe and where everything was kept: shirts, socks, dress-studs, sports kit, ceremonial sword; the while given a run-down on my duties. I was to call him, he instructed me, at 6.50 a.m. sharp with a cup of tea, return after breakfast to make his bunk and clean the cabin. In the evening run his bath, lay out his mess-kit for wardroom dinner, brush and press his number twos and polish his shoes for the morrow. The carpet was to be lifted and the deck scrubbed daily; paintwork washed down once a week. I was also required to launder his 'smalls' – socks, underwear and handkerchiefs – as required. For these services I would receive an emolument of twelve-and-six (62½p) per month, paid quarterly. Officers' servants on their duty-watch days – one evening in four in harbour – reported to the wardroom pantry to assist the stewards with dinner.

It had not escaped my notice, as I took all this in, that the duties of a 'flunkey' were only part-time, and I glumly assumed that the rest of my working day would be spent washing paintwork, or chipping it, or red-leading it. But I was immediately reassured, at least on that point, when Lt Cheyney informed me that I was also to be his yeoman. I followed him up varnished wood and polished brass officer-standard ladders to the chartroom abaft the wheelhouse, trying to look more confident that I felt. I knew that our divisional officer was also the ship's navigating officer, Mick Doherty having mentioned that fact – but surely I couldn't be navigator's yeoman? That was a qualified and highly responsible post, the specialism of a studious AB too brainy for gunnery and not robust enough for torpedoes; the type referred to by his shipmates, with good-humoured contempt, as a 'pie-arse-squared rating'. I knew a little chartwork, as did every AC boy, there being a paper on elementary navigation in the education test second class which we had all taken; but only enough to interpret chart symbols, allow for variation and lay-off a course with parallel ruler and dividers. I feared that this might not be enough, and so it was to prove.

Lt Cheyney pulled open the bank of long, shallow, brass-bound drawers beneath the chart-table. They were crammed with Admiralty charts in numbered folios, contained in brown canvas covers with tie-strings. He pulled one out, dumped it on the table, and extracted a chart. He then handed me a thin, wire-stapled paper booklet; it was headed, in bold black capitals: *Admiralty Notices to Mariners No. 11/48*. He explained that this contained corrections to charts and other Hydrographic Office publications such as tide-tables. Admiralty Notices were issued as required, in practice about once a fortnight, notifying such information as changes in the position or characteristics of navigation buoys and other marks; alterations to the depths of dredged channels or the limits of off-shore gunnery ranges; lighthouses gone dark and many, many more. These were obviously things which affected the safe navigation of a ship in coastal waters and it was important that corrections were effected promptly and charts kept up-to-date. This was to be my job. Stand-easy came and went while the navigating officer demonstrated how to do chart corrections and then got me to

do some, plying ruler, dividers, a mapping-pen and tiny bottles
of different-coloured Indian ink. 'Up spirits' was heard and I
was dying for a cigarette, and then, at last, 'Hands to dinner',
and I was released, Lt Cheyney ordering me to report to the
chartroom for more instruction after 'Hands fall in'.

I returned to the messdeck and questioning from curious and
somewhat envious members of my draft, who had been chipping
paintwork all morning. Dinner was being dished out. I asked one
lad, a conventionally red-haired, raw-boned Scot: 'Where do we
sit?' He regarded me contemptuously.

'Whaur thur's a fookn' space, Jock!'

Most of our new messmates were ex-*Ganges* boys who were
there before us; some were alumni of the other place, HMS *St
Vincent* at Gosport, an alien species. *St James* carried forty boys,
which was a very large number for a destroyer. This was only
partly due to the manpower shortage referred to earlier; it also
owed something to *St James's* reputation, for ships to carry
large numbers of Boy Seamen were carefully selected by the
Sea Lords; clearly they held our ship in high esteem. *St James*
was 'second-leader' of the Fifth Destroyer Flotilla and our
captain was a full commander.

When hands fell-in after dinner and before detailing for work,
special parties – gunner's, boatswain's, messdeck sweepers and
on this occasion, officers' servants – were fallen-out. I stood
anxiously in line with half-a-dozen others, and when we were
ordered to report to the chief steward in the wardroom, ventured
to inform the 'Buffer' that I had previous instructions.

'Don't know anything about that', he said. 'Chief steward – *at
the double*!' I obeyed the last order.

We reported to the wardroom pantry, where the chief petty
officer steward awaited us. He was a short, stout, jolly man with
an air of bustling efficiency. He led us into the wardroom, deserted
at this time of day, lined us up across its width and instructed us
to roll back the heavy carpet. The furniture – heavy, polished oak
table, and dining chairs, leather-covered armchairs – was stacked
against the bulkhead. We were given a bucket each, filled with
scaldingly hot water and a dollop of below-stairs soft soap,
together with scrubber and swab. In desperation I spoke up again,
informing the chief of my double-booking. He was unimpressed.

'This afternoon you're mine, laddie. Sooner you get started, sooner you can go!'

As I sank wearily to my knees, I experienced that feeling of numb helplessness that must be familiar to anyone who has been bottom-of-the-pile in any military, or naval, hierarchy; of being swept along by the whim of higher powers. I was unhappy because I felt that a lieutenant outranked a CPO. I was not to know at that stage that the chief steward ran the wardroom and was not to be crossed by a junior member of it. We scrubbed and swabbed down the considerable length of the room until, exhausted and sweaty, the chief allowed us a stand-easy while the deck dried and the carpet and furniture could be replaced. Then we were dismissed. As I made my belated way to the chartroom I wondered, not for the first time, if my naval career was to be all skivvy-like servitude. I felt cheated – none of the Navy's recruiting posters had shown Jack on his knees, wringing out a grubby deck-swab. He was shown astride a 14-inch gun barrel, wearing snow-white tropical ducks and a cheery grin, polishing his tampion against a background of swaying palms. In fact, a seaman rating in the post-war Navy spent more time on his knees than a revivalist preacher. I looked to my navigator's yeomanhood to take me away from all that.

The chartroom was empty and I ran Mark (as I had come to think of him) down in his cabin, busy at his desk with paperwork. He cut short my explanations – dashing my hope that he would send for the CPO steward and roast him there and then for over-riding his orders – and took me back up top. He set me to more corrections under his supervision until, expressing himself satisfied, he left me to it; not before letting me know what I could see for myself, that a considerable backlog of corrections had accrued. He looked to me to reduce it, quickly, and hinted that navigator's yeomen did not necessarily 'secure' when the pipe went, when there was work to catch up on. So I worked on, missing tea, until it was time to run Mark's bath. While he was taking it, I laid out his evening dress as he had instructed me; mess jacket and trousers freshly brushed and draped on the bunk; boiled shirt on top, dress-studs inserted, wing-collar and black tie; evening shoes dusted and placed side-by-side on the deck with silk socks tucked in; cummerbund ready to hand.

The heady scent of talcum powder and pink gins infiltrated the cabin flat. I went below, to supper.

Subsequently and for several weeks, I spent most of my days, dog-watches included, toiling in the hallowed quiet of the chartroom reducing the backlog of corrections not only to charts but also to various current publications such as *Admiralty Pilots*, involving much plying of scissors and paste. I visited the messdeck only to eat and sleep, which prompted some resentment on the part of the old salts among the boys as I was excused cook-of-the-mess, an unheard-of concession. This made me an instant enemy and butt of the Petty Officer Boy, a big, loud Scouser called Scallion, soon, to my relief, to be rated Ordinary Seaman and shifted forrard. I did my share of washing up, however, in the course of my duty as wardroom pantry-hand; much more of it than on the messdeck, with the crockery, cutlery and glasses from a five-course dinner to wash and polish. I got off to a bad start with the leading steward on my first evening's duty. He was clearing away after dinner when his hand came through the pantry hatch and set down a coffee cup half-full of a clear liquid which I took to be water. I tipped it out and washed the cup. He forgave me eventually, and we got on well, as I never again interfered with his pilfered gin.

Lieutenant Cheyney kept a close eye on progress in the chartroom. I was gradually getting on top of the corrections; a case of two steps forward and one back each time a new *Admiralty Notices* was delivered to the ship. As a Home Fleet ship, *St James* carried a 'suit' of charts which covered the British Isles, near Continent, west to the Azores and south to the western Mediterranean. This amounted to some 250 charts, and there was an obvious temptation – not always resisted as I discovered – to skimp on those further shores not likely to get a visit from us in the foreseeable future. Gradually, even they were brought up to date, and I found myself with spare moments for the other duties falling to the navigator's yeoman. One of these was to keep the ship's clocks showing the correct time. At a few minutes to 9 o'clock each forenoon, I unlocked a drawer in the chartroom and took from it the ship's chronometer. This was a very accurate and delicate timepiece, in appearance like a stop-watch, carefully stowed in its own velvet-lined, brass-bound wooden box with a glass panel set in the lid through which the dial was visible. Carrying this carefully down ladders and along alleyways, I repaired with it to the Wireless Office aft, whose holy ground I was permitted to enter to await the BBC's 9 o'clock time-signal. Under the chief telegraphist's cynical gaze I breathlessly awaited the final, prolonged 'pip' while peering intently at the chronometer's sweep-second hand, mentally noting any discrepancy. Tucked in the box with the instrument was a printed form on which I noted the date and any seconds or fractions thereof fast or slow. I then wound it. It was emphatically not permitted to attempt any adjustment to the chronometer; if it should fail to keep time to within two seconds, it was despatched to the Hydrographical Depot for overhaul.

This morning ceremony performed, I did a lightning tour of the wardroom, captain's sea and day-cabins and the bridge, adjusting clocks as necessary.

All this time, St James remained firmly attached to the dockyard wall. We had assumed, following our spell in salt-stained Ulster, that we could expect to put to sea at least once a week. But in 1948 sea-time, like most other things, was strictly rationed and it was not just concern for our sparkling paintwork that kept St James in harbour, 'aground on 'er own milk-tins', as Slinger Woods claimed.

We boys did enjoy a brief break with routine on Whit Saturday when our DO hired a coach, courtesy of the ship's canteen fund, to take us to the Dartmoor Hunt point-to-point meeting near, I think, Widecombe. We paraded in the waist in number twos and lanyards, clutching the ineluctable bag-meals, as our coach drew on to the jetty, and awaited with impatience our divisional officer. After several minutes, my neighbour nudged me and breathed, 'Christ – what have you done to your bloke?' I turned my head to behold the officer for whose appearance I was responsible approaching. A titter, as they say, ran through the ranks. Lieutenant The Honourable Mandeville-Cheyney RN, who was hoping to be offered a spare mount at the meeting, had with aristocratic insouciance togged himself out in a rig of which I hotly denied any prior knowledge. He was arrayed in, starting at the top, the naval officer's shore-going brown soft hat, tweed hacking-jacket, cord breeches, stiff brown leather leggings like those which pony-and-trap milkmen used to wear, and black parade boots. From his bony wrist dangled a riding-crop. We had a very enjoyable day out and were grateful to him, but were denied the pleasure of seeing him taking the jumps, for no hunt member would lend him a horse, which was perhaps not surprising.

A few days later the pipe 'Special sea-dutymen to your stations' was heard in *St James* and the vibration of her main engines felt beneath the feet. We were not going far: just out of the Sound, turn left, round Prawle Point, left again and up the River Dart to Britannia Royal Naval College, to perform the same service for a party of junior cadets as *Cowdray* had done for 141 class at Shotley; providing a first taste of life in a warship. It was also my first opportunity to help my master prepare for a sea voyage, even one as short as this. The previous evening after supper I had reported to the chartroom to find him busy with tide-tables and charts. This was an anxious business for the navigating officer; any error made in his calculations which hazarded the ship or, worse, put it aground would inevitably result in court-martial. The captain would take the rap, of course, but the NO would go down with him. Not that this trip held many terrors; a reasonably intelligent AB could have accomplished it. But the preparations were routinely thorough and I was kept busy next morning as the ship came to life, equipping the bridge chart-table with the appropriate charts in the required order, freshly sharpened pencils, indiarubber, plotting instruments and the deck-watch, a bargain basement version of the chronometer. On leaving harbour and, on this occasion, throughout the short voyage, I was stationed at the back of the bridge, in case something needed fetching. The only requirement was for a cup of coffee; the captain's steward brought one up for the captain and I brought one for Mark.

We embarked the cadets and headed down-Channel into a loppy sea. Our visitors were shown round the ship as we had been on our first morning in *Ulster*, a seeming age ago. To my glee, they also had to exercise 'Away seaboat', and made a considerable dog's breakfast of it, in spite of having a leading seaman embarked with them. As the day drew on the weather worsened and soon the upper deck was being secured and lifelines rigged. We were running down to Finisterre and into the Bay of Biscay – not solely for the cadets' edification but also to do some rough-weather steaming to test some modification or other to the engines. The cadets were accommodated in an empty messdeck next to ours in the after-flat which would have been a seamen's mess had *St James* the seamen to fill it. By suppertime most of the cadets had turned in. I myself was rapidly losing interest and was thankful that it was not my night for pantry duty. Mark was OOW on the bridge for the last dog and the officers did not dress for dinner at sea, so I was free to sling my hammock.

As I went up top to the bathroom, I saw three or four of my messmates leaning over the open hatchway above the cadets' mess and much nudging and sniggering going on. Wondering what it was all about, I joined the group and peered down. Lying in his hammock directly below, slung across the ladder, was a white-faced, tousle-haired cadet, a mere child of thirteen or so. Dangling just below his nose was a lump of rancid bacon-fat, swinging from a length of cod-line held by 'Larry' Lamb, the boys' mess skate who was always in the rattle. Becoming aware, no doubt, of yet another nauseous shipboard stench, the cadet's eyelids fluttered open, then widened in horror as he gave a little squeal. His complexion changed from dough-grey to pea-green, matching exactly his officer's-issue pyjamas. At that moment the Coxswain entered the flat, going about his occasional law-and-order perambulations, and took in the situation at a glance. He marched us up to the bridge, ignoring my protest that I was just passing by. We were hustled into line at the back of the bridge, where hours before I had proudly stood as a member of the navigation department, now a defaulter. The Captain happened to be on the bridge and asked what was going on. When the Coxswain told him, he sent us below to fetch our hammocks. We were then ordered to the top of the 'Director', a pillbox-like structure high up above the bridge from where the gun turrets were controlled in action. We squatted there, cold and wet from spray in a rising gale, clutching our hammocks, for two hours before being ordered down to turn in. We were left in no doubt that what was a boyish prank when inflicted on a messmate was something prejudicial to good order and naval discipline if the victim happened to be an officer, however embryonic. We were lucky at that; in some ships it would have been six cuts.

Our next sea voyage was in early summer, when we steamed all the way to North Woolwich on the Thames. *St James*, favourite of the Commander-in-Chief Plymouth, had been selected to transport some of Devonport division's teams to the annual Royal Tournament at Olympia. We were to remain for two weeks. On the programme at that time was a tug-of-war contest between the three port divisions and the Fleet Air Arm; a kind of second-feature to the famous field gun event. By a happy chance, our chief petty officers' mess was the heaviest in the Fleet, the twelve of them tipping the scales at a little under a ton, and that included two starvelings. It was therefore decided that the entire Devonport team should be drawn from our ship, as it was economical and convenient for training sessions.

The chiefs had been training assiduously for weeks. As a gesture in the direction of fitness-training, they put in a short daily bout of half-hearted and elephantine shuffling on the fo'c'sle, clad in plimsolls and the largest-obtainable pusser's gym shorts fitted with gussets, while the officer of the day kept an anxious eye on his mooring lines. Sensibly, they did most of their training on the rope. A contraption was rigged in the waist consisting of a cluster of dummy depth-charges filled with concrete and shackled together to a wire strop, from which a heavy mooring rope was led through a pulley-block overhead and ranged along the deck. Shrilly exhorted by their coach, Leading Signalman 'Nellie' Dean, a PTI manqué, they alternately hauled and lay back, with much loud grunting and grimacing. Watching their performance from the gun-decks, we reckoned the trophy was as good as ours, and so it proved.

There was no suitable berth available alongside, with London a busy commercial port in those days, and we moored to buoys out in the river. Following the deleterious effect of the Biscay run on our brass and paintwork, *St James* had rapidly been restored to her customary yacht-like condition, and on several occasions during our visit the ship was made open to visitors. Prior to this, Mark had instructed me to remove anything portable from the bridge, wheelhouse and chartroom and lock them away; I thought I had done this. But soon after a school party from somewhere in Docklands had been aboard it was discovered that the deck-watch was missing, and I had to admit that I must have overlooked it, out of sight as it was under the bridge chart-table. The police were informed and late that evening I was turned out of my hammock, told to put an oilskin on over my pyjamas and report to the wardroom. There I was introduced to a portly, middle-aged detective sergeant with an amiable smile who invited me to go with him to the bridge and show him where the deck-watch was normally kept. He briefly inspected the empty brass case, and then chatted for a few minutes on general topics; clearly passing a little time and 'going through the motions'. No doubt he had had a lot of dealings with London dockers and their progeny and entertained no serious hopes of recovering the watch. It was a balmy evening, with shimmering lights reflected in the smooth, oily Thames, the ebb tide bubbling and gurgling down our ship's side; a pleasant enough interlude. We climbed down from the bridge and parted cordially, he to the wardroom for a farewell gin; me to my hammock.

The fact remained that an item of naval stores could not be accounted for, and that meant that an official inquiry had to be held and blame apportioned. When the time came and I was piped to report to the ship's office, to be marched in by the Coxswain and confront the first lieutenant seated behind the desk, my apprehension was only slightly lessened when I was ordered *sotto voce* to salute, and not 'Off cap', which meant I was not a defaulter – yet. Mark formally testified that he had given me a direct order to remove the deck-watch to a safe place and I admitted that I had received such an order and failed to carry it out. I was plainly culpable and it remained only to refer to the stores rate book to determine that the value of an Admiralty pattern deck-watch was 30 shillings (£1.50) and that this sum would be paid by me in restitution. I was then dismissed, relieved that there was no more punitive penalty but reflecting ruefully that on a Boy Seaman's pay I would receive a 'Nor-Easter' (not entitled) on the next two fortnightly paydays. However, Mark followed me out and told me that he would pay a pound towards it, leaving me to find the odd ten bob, which was very decent of him if it was his own idea, though I suspected the first lieutenant might have had a word.

A few days later, there was a further development. The captain's secretary, a young, earnest supply lieutenant who had been present at the inquiry in charge of the rate book, decided to delve into his bible, *King's Regulations and Admiralty Instructions*, and discovered that the only item of permanent stores (that is, as distinct from consumable stores such as paint-brushes and bars of pusser's hard) for which a boy could be held responsible was a bosun's call. So I was let off and Mark, presumably, had to pay the full cost. I felt badly about it, and feared that it might put my 'quiet number' as navvie's yeoman at risk, but nothing more was said; no doubt it was accepted as a consequence of putting a boy to do a man's job.

My days in the chartroom were numbered in any case. Summer leave was not far off and a few weeks after that, I reached the magic age of seventeen-and-a-half and would 'shift forrard' on rating to Ordinary Seaman. That would be the end of my 'quiet number', for I would thereafter be just another upper-deck hand, working ship and keeping watches. There also loomed the prospect of some serious sea time at last; *St James* was to take part in the Home Fleet's autumn cruise to the Mediterranean. That meant, for me, a sustained and frenetic bout of chart-correcting, dusting off folios from the bottom drawer, undisturbed since delivery from the Chart Depot, with Mark hovering over me anxiously. He actually suggested that I should bring my bedding up and sleep on the chartroom bunk. I was relieved to be allowed to proceed on summer leave with the rest of the ship's company.

END OF SEAMAN BOYHOOD

Soon after return from Long Leave, we left the Dockyard and steamed round to Wembury Point, just outside the Sound, and tied up to the long wooden jetty of the Ammunition Depot. There were large red 'Danger' and 'No Smoking' signs everywhere. Before arrival all smoking materials – cigarettes, pipes, matches and lighters – were collected by the Coxswain and locked away. As soon as we were secured the pipe 'Clear lower deck, ammunition ship' was heard. 'Ammunition ship' was an evolution akin to the old, loathed 'Coal ship' that some of our stripeys still spoke of, though not nearly so dirty and much less frequent. This was Mr Duncan the commissioned gunner's show, for which he and his party had been preparing for days, but which, like coaling, involved the entire ship's company except men on watch, including officers and, of course, the navigator's yeoman.

Soon a squat, waddling, heavy-laden ammunition lighter, distinguished by the broad red band around its black hull, came out from shore and secured alongside. I was one of a party of boys ordered over the side to remove hatch-covers and rig the derrick. We stayed in the lighter to unload: first, deep in the lighter's bowels, lifting 4.5-inch shells into a tubular steel cradle, four rounds at a time, to be hooked-on and hoisted inboard for stowage in the magazines fore and aft. This was back-breaking work and took the whole forenoon. We climbed wearily inboard for dinner, after which a pipe was made to the effect that a smoking area would be open in the canteen flat for fifteen minutes. There was a rush forward which included me, but by the time I had queued at the coxswain's office to retrieve my cigarettes, I had only time for a couple of puffs before 'Out pipes' went. Then back down in the lighter, where for the rest of the day and well into the dog-watches, we unloaded heavy steel cases of Bofors and small-arms ammunition and bombs for our 'Squid' anti-submarine mortar abaft the fo'c'sle. When at length the lighter was empty and all explosives struck below, we cast off and returned to our bit of dockyard wall, ready for storing ship the next day. Aching in every limb, we could at least reflect that after humping 500 4.5-inch projectiles, sacks of spuds and cases of tinned milk held no terrors for us.

Store ship went on up to the eve of sailing. Unlike the ammunitioning, I was excused this exercise and was back in the chart room, with my master the navigating officer squeezing the last drops of effort from me before my rating-up. However, he happened to be officer of the day when the rum-lorry arrived alongside, and whenever the rum store was opened the OOD was required to be present. He took me down with him to assist. The rum store was situated right aft in the ship, down in the bilges below the tiller flat, a space housing the steering machinery. Access was gained via a small steel hatch, heavily butterfly-clipped and padlocked. This straitened opening was a considerable embarrassment to our Coxswain, one of the gargantuan members of the *St James* CPOs' mess who had effortlessly carried away the Royal Tournament tug-of-war trophy. He had never actually entered this small but important part of his fiefdom; at the daily 'Up spirits' contenting himself instead with peering in from the flat above while a minion tapped off the day's issue. He was there now, swinging his big bunch of keys. He saluted Mark, as did Scouse Allard, the Sick Berth Attendant with his first-aid satchel slung. King's Regulations and Admiralty Instructions laid it down that an SBA must always be in attendance when hands were working in the rum store, in case anyone was overcome by exposure to fumes. This did not apply to daily issues, when such exposure was of short duration. Or to actually drinking the stuff.

I was sent down to aid a supply assistant, who was pouring rum from the wicker-covered stone jars in which it was supplied, into the bung-hole of a brass-bound cask securely clamped on chocks. The atmosphere in the cramped little compartment was indeed heady. Highly polished brass and copper glittered in the light from a single small bulb in the deckhead. I was in the holy of holies of the naval rum cult, surrounded by its sacred vessels. There was a set of elegant, round-bellied, broad-lipped copper jugs, all exactly identical in shape but ranging in size from the huge two-gallon down to a dear little one-gill like a cream jug. Beside the big cask was clamped the barricoe (pronounced breaker), a smart little varnished barrel not round but oval in cross-section, with brass hoops and padlocked bung-hole, all brightly polished. This was used every day to bring up the daily issue, to be poured into the rum tub for mixing with 'two-water' after the chief and petty officers' 'neaters' had been drawn off. The rum tub itself, though destroyer-size rather than battleship-size, was too big for the rum store and was stowed in the after-flat, near to the quarterdeck from whence issues were made. This receptacle is the one probably most familiar to the reader: a large round tub broader at the base than the rim and emblazoned with big brass letters spelling out 'The King God Bless Him'. Most rum tubs had been in service for many years, being returned to stores when ships paid off and reissued to new ships on commissioning, so when in February 1952 'K's, 'I's, 'G's and 'M's throughout the

Fleet were unscrewed and returned to store, being replaced by the appropriate 'Q's, 'U's, 'E's and 'R's, it may not have been for the first time. (Following the last issue of Royal Navy rum at the end of July 1970, the Admiralty sold off all these magnificent appurtenances, many of them to naval officers serving and retired, who were given preference; this seems unfair as they were Jack's utensils, after all. No doubt they will soon begin to appear at *Antiques Roadshows* in Winchester, Fleet and Budleigh Salterton).

The captain cleared lower deck and we mustered aft to be briefed on the forthcoming cruise. We were to take part in anti-submarine exercises and gunnery shoots in the eastern Atlantic, extending towards but not quite up to the Azores, and in the Bay of Biscay. On completion *St James*, favoured as always, was to accompany the flagship (the aircraft-carrier *Theseus* borrowed from the Mediterranean Fleet) to Madeira, while the rest of the Fleet visited Lisbon. This news meant little to us boys but the 'old bastards' were delighted by it, assuring everyone that Funchal was 'the best fuckin' run ashore in the Med!'

We unberthed on a muggy, grey September morning and steamed down the Sound in a light drizzle. Clear of the fairway, we rendezvoused with our sister-ships of the Fifth Flotilla and proceeded down-Channel in company. Out of the Channel chops and south into the Bay, the weather was a good deal kinder than it had been on our last visit to those waters. There was a long, slow swell rolling in from the Atlantic which caused our narrow-gutted destroyers to roll sluggishly 15 or 20° to each beam. This made life difficult, with any loose gear skidding about, and it was tiring, bracing oneself against the motion all the time; but I for one much preferred it to the sickening, jarring pitch known as 'scending', which I had got to know so well in the Pentland Firth. On the second day out we came within gun-range of the 'enemy', some units of the Mediterranean Fleet who had emerged from the Straits of Gibraltar to join battle with us. *St James*, together with two of our sisters, *Sluys* and *Agincourt*, led a submarine-hunt against one of the Med Fleet's 'T'-class boats, and after a whole day and a night of much high-speed manoeuvring and Asdic-pinging, culminating in a spectacular salvo from our ahead-firing 'Squid' mortar, claimed a 'kill'. We then rejoined the Fleet for gunnery shoots.

My action-station was deep down in the ship, in a small compartment known as the transmitting station, or 'TS'. A small group of us under the gunner's mate clustered about the fire control table, an early form of mechanical computer, twiddling the various knobs and dials which collected data on an enemy ship's course and speed, angles of elevation and deflection and sundry other calculations. This information was fed to the guns via the director, so that all four turrets ranged on the same point. My own job in this team was quite important: that of receiving 'fall of shot' information from the director high above the bridge and passing in return corrected firing orders. It was a duty normally carried out by a highly trained and qualified gunnery rating, but there was a dearth of these among St James's complement, in common with most ships at that time. I had received a few hours' instruction from our gunnery officer while on passage from Plymouth. These sessions took place in Mark's cabin, with the GO and me seated on opposite settees. The GO held on his lap a board about two feet square. It had a little model of a ship at one edge and rows of keys like a typewriter down the other. When one of these keys was depressed a steel rivet popped up through a hole drilled in the board; this represented the waterspout thrown up by a shell. The gunnery officer explained everything and told me what orders to give so that ranging was corrected and a straddle achieved. He would pop up some rivets and I would order 'Up two hundred, zig-zag shoot' or some such redress, whereupon the rivets would drop out of sight and a fresh lot appear, corrected for line. It was rather more complicated than that, but the reader will get the gist. After a few such sessions, the GO expressed himself satisfied, though looking, I thought, a little doubtful, and posted me to the duties of a gunlayer second class. I do not wish to give the impression that I was some sort of Boy Seaman-prodigy, as this was not the case; many other boys were hastily trained to do men's jobs, including my oppo Pete Salkeld who was appointed director-layer, an even more vital post. Chief Gunner's Mate Blenkinsop would have been proud of us, if incredulous.

The exercises lasted for sixteen days. Halfway through this, the time came for me to complete a 'request chit', on which I formally petitioned to 'see the Captain through the First Lieutenant to be rated Ordinary Seaman'. This was the laid-down form of procedure; one always asked to see the captain 'through' the first lieutenant, though the first hurdle was, of course, the coxswain. He took my request-chit and studied it with an air of simulated incredulity that I was aspiring to man's estate, told me to report to the leading hand of Five Mess after rating and warned me not to be adrift when 'Captain's requestmen' was piped.

After twenty months' boy's service, it all happened very quickly and without much ceremony. I was marched before the captain, saluting smartly; he looked up from my service history sheet which the secretary had slid on to his blotter and eyed me shrewdly but benignly:

'Well Phillipson, this is a big step for you. I'm told you've been doing well – keep it up! A word of advice: *joie de vivre* is a very good thing to have, so long as you don't overdo it, do you understand me?'

'Yessir, thank you sir', I lied, not understanding at all. He was obviously confusing me with another boy, any other boy. I assumed he had been badly briefed.

'Rated Ordinary Seaman. Thank you, Coxswain, who's next?' I saluted again and withdrew, with a sense of anticlimax. Strictly, this account should end here as our subject is Boy Seamen and I no longer was one, but the consequent changes to my daily existence were great and deserve recording. I had done no handing-over of my twin duties of officer's servant and navigator's yeoman: the first was taken care of by the arrival of two officers' stewards from RNB the day we left Plymouth, and the charts were more-or-less up to date for the time being. Anyway, they were no longer my problem.

I hauled my kitbag and hammock forrard to Five Mess, one of four broadside messes on the main seamen's messdeck. At dinner-time I 'made my number' with 'Tug' Wilson, killick of the mess, who found me an empty seat-locker and spare hammock-billet. He also added my name to the duty-cook rota, with my cooking oppo a senior AB, Ron Eason, member of the boatswain's party who looked after the paint-store in the forepeak. This was a considerable relief to me as ship's company messes were on the canteen messing system, and I knew nothing of the art of pastry-making. I reported again to the Coxswain, who issued me with a new station card which placed me in the second part of the starboard watch. We were at sea, so my watchkeeping began at once: I was again lucky as my 'part of watch' had the last dog that day and 'all night in'. The gunner's mate, chronically short-handed, had anticipated my rating-up and on the strength of my honorary gunnery rating, grabbed me ahead of the other petty officers for the gunner's party. So I now had a part of watch, a cooking-chum and, I hoped, a quiet number in a special party. Any feelings I might have had of amounting to something were quickly dispelled on the messdeck, where it was made clear that I was just another 'fuckin' OD', lumped together with a handful of green youths enlisted as adults and fresh from a ten-week course in barracks. This was probably deliberate policy, designed to keep ex-boys from playing 'Jack-me-hearty', which we might have been inclined to do.

I was looking forward to my first pay-day. On rating ordinary seaman from boy, pay leapt from a few shillings to fifty shillings every fortnight. There were two reasons for this spectacular increase: the normal increment of pay for a higher rating, and the discontinuance of a boy's allotment. The Admiralty in their wisdom decreed that a proportion – the larger proportion, in fact – of a boy's pay should be held back and allotted by him to his parents, next-of-kin, or in the case of those with no-one in the world, a savings bank. On rating, the ex-boy was allowed to keep all his pay to spend as he wished. I had nominated my mother as beneficiary of my seven shillings (35p) weekly. She had never mentioned this bounty and neither had I; inasmuch as I gave it a thought, I supposed it went to the housekeeping budget. But on my next home leave after rating my mother triumphantly handed me a tallyman's book with twenty months-worth of seven shillingses religiously entered therein, and was held to my credit at a men's outfitters of the 'natty gents' sort in our local high street. I had little need for civilian clothes – at that date, HM Forces on leave were not allowed to wear them, just as in wartime – and I don't know what possessed her. (When I was aboard *Ulster*, persuaded of some entirely imaginary interest on my part in parliamentary democracy, she had taken out a subscription for me to the weekly *Hansard*. It caused a raised eyebrow or two from officers of the day on evening rounds who saw me reading it in my hammock.) However, the accumulated funds had to be spent, as did an entire morning being fitted out with the regulation fawn belted raincoat of that day and a double-breasted pin-stripe suit of a purplish colour. Having exhausted the shop's main stock-range and still with several pounds in hand, in desperation I found myself buying exotic items of apparel that I would never wear and that would barely serve as Christmas presents, such as polka-dot cravats and sock-suspenders.

Other benefits of ordinary seamanship were that I could opt out of Divine Service and was allowed shore-leave, when granted, until 2359 hours, like Cinderella.

My man's service got off to a bad start. I had considerable difficulty in getting to sleep in Five Mess; not something which had troubled me before. Exactly in the middle of the messdeck and directly beneath my hammock (which was no doubt why that particular billet had been vacant) was a piece of machinery called the hull and fire pump. It was a steel cylinder about two feet in diameter and four high, painted battleship grey and festooned with brass piping which, being on a messdeck, was kept brightly polished by the mess-deck sweeper. Its function, I believe, was to maintain the necessary pressure in the ship's fire main. It was designed to switch itself on and off as necessary, running for as little as ten minutes or as much as an hour at a time, and was extremely noisy. Old hands assured me I would get used to it and after a time would not be aware of it. This proved to be the case, but it took many weeks. In the meantime, it kept me awake for an hour or more after turning in; either listening to its high-pitched whine or waiting tensely for it to switch in.

On my fourth night in the mess I turned in early as I had the middle watch, midnight to 4 a.m. I eventually got to sleep and remembered nothing more until 'Call the hands'. I realized that I had slept through my middle watch; a messmate in my watch assured me that I had not been missed, and I congratulated myself on a gash 'all night in'. This was premature: when we mustered in the waist for the first dog under Leading Seaman

'Jan' Treharne, a morose, acidulous individual with a deep hatred
for ODs, who had only the previous day joined our part of watch
and had not been aware until now that I belonged to it – he
demanded to know why I had been adrift the previous night. My
lame excuse that the hull and fire pump had kept me awake and
that I must have slept through the pipe and the 'shake' from the
first watch bosun's mate did not impress him. He could have 'put
me in the rattle' and had me up as a defaulter, 'Absent place of
duty, conduct prejudicial to good order and naval discipline',
thereby blotting my hitherto spotless record; instead, he detailed
me for life-buoy sentry, and I made my way to the quarterdeck
for a solitary two-hour watch.

The watch on deck at night was deployed thus: two bridge
messengers doing two hours each; four look-outs changed every
hour and two lifebuoy sentries normally doing a two-hour spell
each. The remainder of the watch formed the emergency
seaboat's crew, which meant they found a warm spot on the
engine-room hatches near the whaler; smoked, spun yarns and
drank cocoa until it was time to 'shake' the next watch. The
lifebuoy sentry found what shelter he could on a windy and
usually wet quarterdeck within earshot of the bridge alarm gong
which would indicate 'Man overboard', alone and with plenty of
time to reflect on the injustice meted out to an OD who 'didn't
hear the pipe'. For that was my punishment – lifebuoy sentry on
every nightwatch, for the entire watch, for the rest of the cruise.
I would rather have been in the rattle.

Making pastry, standing watches, shore-leave in sultry foreign
ports and money to spend – all these delights and more awaited
the boy newly released from his instructor's tender care to the
impartial hurly-burly of a seamen's mess and the amiable disdain
of senior hands for a lowly OD. He learned to stand on his own
feet and employ better excuses than 'I didn't hear the pipe'. He
thought he knew it all, and was often led into temptation, for he
was still of callow years. Let the last word be had by Thomas
Holman who we encountered earlier, joining as a boy in 1872
and 'coming up through the hawsepipe' via gunner to lieutenant:

It is at the age of from eighteen to twenty-one that all the
dangers of a young man's career in the navy confront him.

Recently let loose from the close supervision that used to be, and still is, excercised over boys, and becoming entitled to be rated as a man on the ship's books, together with receiving different treatment from all the men around him, and being allowed his grog, it is seldom indeed that a young man has sufficient ballast on board to steady him in such a sea of excitement. . . . If a lad can but tide over his first two or three years of manhood, without getting into serious trouble, his position is comparatively safe.[5]

Few ex-Boy Seamen would dispute Mr Holman's view, but that is another story. . . .

Postscript

On New Year's Eve 1954, a new captain arrived at Shotley. Captain Michael Le Fanu DSC, RN was young (the youngest captain in the Navy List), brilliant and unconventional; a man for his time at a point when the Royal Navy was at last starting to catch up with the mid twentieth century. HMS *Ganges* had typically been commanded by crusty naval dinosaurs at the end of their active careers, officers who as midshipmen might well have led a boatload of bluejackets armed with cutlasses through the surf on some tropical shore, personifications of the yawning gulf between wardroom and lower deck.

'Ginger' Le Fanu was appalled by what he found, and resolved on sweeping changes from top to bottom of the establishment. Without any relaxation of discipline he, by his own example of informality – strolling around the barracks in civilian clothes without the captain's usual retinue, stopping boys to chat to them, refereeing their games, going sailing with them clad in jersey and shorts – directed the officers' and instructors' attention to other than what he himself called 'the boys' socks attitude'. It was nothing less than a revolution; the captain of *Ganges* had always been a remote and God-like figure to the boys, glimpsed only as he swept past at captain's rounds or Divisions and never directly addressed by him unless as defaulters at his table.

Changes such as these once made, cannot be reversed, and after Michael Le Fanu moved on at the end of his two-year appointment to continue his upward progress all the way to First Sea Lord, head of his Service, Shotley, for the few years remaining to its long, formidable history, was a different place.

On 1 April 1956 the rating of boy in the Royal Navy was abolished, ending three centuries of tradition. At the same time the scope of entry for fifteen-year-olds was widened to include, as well as the seaman branch, engineering, electrical and Fleet Air Arm. They were now known on entry as Junior Seaman 2nd class, or Junior Engineering or Electrical Mechanic as appropriate.

Further changes were necessarily made to accommodate extension to school-leaving age, until juvenile recruitment virtually ceased and the establishment was closed in 1973.

> And I still look back with gratitude and admiration to the Royal Naval Training Establishment at Shotley. As was to be expected, it strengthened me physically, but above all it provided a firm moral basis and wide mental vistas which no other school for a boy of my class could have given. If, after almost forty years' absence, I visit or return to Britain, I shall go pay homage to the school I believe to be – in fact am absolutely convinced is – the best in the world.

A tribute from one of those exceedingly rare flag-officers who began their careers as Boy Seamen? Not quite. It was written in valedictory mood by one ex-Able Seaman Len Wincott, Communist and leader of the notorious Invergordon Mutiny, from exile in his Moscow flat at the age of sixty-six.

Other sweeping changes took place in the service at large, as if the Admiralty was awakening from the long dream of its past. The rum ration, as we have seen, was abolished; with a new generation of warships on the drawing-board, naval constructors were enjoined to give some consideration to men's living-spaces so that there was room for bunks and Jack's hammock could be consigned to history where it belonged, likewise the archaic canteen messing system with the provision of cafetarias. And the siting of noisy machinery elsewhere than the middle of a seaman's sleeping-space!

One recent development is beyond the reach of an old sailor's comprehension – female officers and ratings serving alongside men in warships at sea. Kiss me, Hardy.

Notes

CHAPTER ONE

1 So called because these officers, together with the purser and cook, were appointed by warrant to a specific ship and, in theory at least, remained with it throughout its life, including periods when out of commission or refitting.
2 Two centuries later, an 'upperyardman' was a rating selected for officer training.
3 David Howarth, *Trafalgar, the Nelson Touch*, Collins, 1969.
4 Watered rum ('grog') was issued to boys until 1851. Later, in 1881, issue was restricted to men over twenty, which regulation remained until the rum issue was abolished on 31 July 1970.
5 Quoted in Howarth, *Trafalgar*.
6 *A Voice from the Main Deck*, Boston, USA, 1843.
7 *Life on board a Man-of-War*, 1829.
8 From an unpublished journal lent by Frederick Stokes and quoted by Henry Baynham in *From the Lower Deck*, Hutchinson, 1969.
9 The 'hidebound' British Army had introduced regular engagements nearly a century earlier.

CHAPTER TWO

1 Charles Humphrey, *Recollections*, quoted by H. Baynham in *Before the Mast*, Hutchinson, 1971.
2 Thomas Holman, *Life in the Royal Navy*, G. Chamberlain, Portsmouth, 1891.
3 A single, prolonged bugle-note in the key of G.
4 Oral record, quoted by Baynham in *Men from the Dreadnoughts*, Hutchinson, 1976.
5 Sam Noble, *'Tween-decks in the Seventies*, Sampson Low, 1926.

CHAPTER THREE

1   John Bechervaise, *Thirty-six Years of Seafaring*.
2   Ralph Westacott. From the Sound Recording Archive of Henry Baynham, copies of which are held by the Imperial War Museum in London.
3   'Gobbies' was the nickname for coastguards. By this date, with the diminution in smuggling, the coastguard's main function was as an active naval reserve, its members interchangeable with Fleet personnel.
4   Ralph Westacott. From the Sound Recording Archive of Henry Baynham.
5   Ibid.
6   William Prayle. From the Sound Recording Archive of Henry Baynham.
7   and following passages, H.J. Austin. From the Sound Recording Archive of Henry Baynham.
8   In a wooden-wall, the lowest deck, lying on or below the waterline.
9   Jack delighted in mocking the food he was given: a kipper was 'Spithead Pheasant'; bacon and tinned tomato 'Tram-smash'; fried egg on toast 'Marine on a Raft'.
10 Anon. *The Seamen of the Royal Navy, the Advantages and Disadvantages as viewed from the Lower Deck*, 1877.
11 Until 1923, a member of the Royal Marine Artillery as distinct from the Royal Marine Light Infantry ('Red Marine').
12 George Crowland. From the Sound Recording Archive of Henry Baynham.
13 Bertram Kiel. Ibid.
14 Henry Minchin. Ibid.
15 William Gardner. Ibid.
16 George Kimbell. Ibid.
17 A seamen's mess as distinct from an 'enclosed mess' usually allocated to boys. Dates from the wooden walls where the seamen had their messes between the broadside guns.
18 George Crowland. From the Sound Recording Archive of Henry Baynham.
19 Frank Adams. Ibid.
20 George Crowland. Ibid.
21 From *Invergordon Scapegoat*, a biography of Admiral

Tomkinson by Alan Coles, Alan Sutton, 1993.
22 HMS *Mars* was a pre-Dreadnought battleship and lacked fitted steel coal chutes. Canvas chutes were rigged which were ill-fitting and allowed coal-dust to escape and settle on decks and paintwork.
23 William Broadway. From the Sound Recording Archive of Henry Baynham.

CHAPTER FOUR

1 Known derisively at Shotley as 'nozzers'. This term, origin unknown, is of ancient lineage and was in use at least as far back as 1790.
2 Hollywood musical star of the 1940s.
3 Cheap cigarettes, known as 'coffin nails'. Until the 1947 Budget, these could be bought in the NAAFI canteen at twenty for a shilling (5p).
4 After initial issue the naval rating purchased his own uniform. No self-respecting sailor would buy his clothing from 'slops', but would be measured for a new suit at one of the naval tailors located at the major ports. 'Bernards of Harwich' was probably the most famous; Jack's answer to Gieves.

CHAPTER FIVE

1 Ralph Westacott. From the Sound Recording Archive of Henry Baynham, copies of which are held by the Imperial War Museum in London.
2 Charles Cutler. Ibid.
3 Ibid.
4 Bertram Kiel. Ibid.
5 Thomas Holman. Ibid.

POSTSCRIPT

1 Len Wincott, *Invergordon Mutineer,* Weidenfeld & Nicolson, 1974.

Bibliography

Baker, Richard. *'Dry Ginger', Biography of Admiral of the Fleet Sir Michael Le Fanu*, W.H. Allen, 1977

Baynham, Henry. *'From the Lower Deck': The Old Navy 1780–1840*, Hutchinson, 1969

——. *'Before the Mast': Naval Ratings of the 19th Century*, Hutchinson, 1971

——. *Men from the Dreadnoughts*, Hutchinson, 1976

Coles, Alan and Briggs, Ted. *Flagship 'Hood'*, Robert Hale, 1985

Divine, David. *Mutiny at Invergordon*, MacDonald, 1970

Hampshire, A. Cecil. *The Royal Navy since 1945*, William Kimber, 1975

Howarth, David. *Trafalgar, The Nelson Touch*, Collins, 1969

Keegan, John. *The Price of Admiralty*, Hutchinson, 1988

Laffin, John. *Jack Tar, the Story of the British Sailor*, Cassell, 1969

Masefield, John. *Sea Life in Nelson's Time*, Conway Maritime, 1905; Sphere Books, 1972

Roger, N.A.M. *The Wooden World, An Anatomy of the Georgian Navy*, Fontana, 1988

Webb, John. *'Way Aloft!' The History of the HMS 'Ganges' Mast*, Willis Faber, 1990

Wincott, Len. *Invergordon Mutineer*, Weidenfeld & Nicolson, 1974

OTHER SOURCES

Articles in Brassey's *Naval Annual* 1937–39 by Cdr H. Pursey RN

'Diary of a Young Seaman' by C.M. Macklen, in the *Naval Review*, 1935

Sound Recording Archive of the Imperial War Museum, by permission of Mr Henry Baynham

Index